Hashicorp Terraform Associate Certification (Exam 003)

Upskill and certify your IT infrastructure automation skills with this exam-cum-study guide

Kimiko Lee

Published by: GitforGits

Publisher: Sonal Dhandre

www.gitforgits.com

support@gitforgits.com

Printed in India

First Printing: October 2023

ISBN: 9788119177295

Cover Design by: Kitten Publishing

Prologue

This is the beginning of a significant learning journey that will hopefully help you become a master of Terraform. Terraform is a game-changing technology for managing infrastructure as code, and this book will show you what you need to know to become an expert or a certified user. Whether you're on-premises, in the cloud, or using a combination of the two, Terraform gives you the ability to code and manage your infrastructure just like software development. This book will help you get ready for HashiCorp's Terraform Certification, which signifies your competence in this field, by providing both theoretical background and practical tasks.

Skilled Terraform practitioners are in high demand due to the platform's great potential and its widespread adoption in the IT industry. The way we plan for, implement, and oversee infrastructure management has undergone a sea change, and this technology is at the vanguard of that change. Using a declarative language, Terraform eliminates the need for ad hoc scripts or manual setups and instead generates code that is concise, easy to understand, and reusable. This book is an attempt to encapsulate that spirit by providing a systematic, all-encompassing way to learn Terraform, beginning with the fundamentals and on to more complex subjects.

We start by taking a deep dive into Terraform's fundamental architecture, learning all about its providers, resources, and state files. As we go along, we'll use real-life examples and scenarios to bolster the theoretical notions. A lot of them will be set in the framework of CloudOptic, a made-up but totally genuine tech business. The ability to develop code that is both reusable and easy to maintain is essential for any infrastructure project, and you will learn how to use Terraform modules to accomplish just that. Module types and their practical applications are covered extensively, with a special emphasis on root, child, and published modules.

We go beyond providing the bare minimum in terms of infrastructure. The book walks you through the ins and outs of Terraform's more complex features and capabilities, including manipulating states, conditional logic, and dependencies. In order to manage complicated, enterprise-level infrastructures, these subjects are essential. You'll also find out how to deal with configuration drift, a critical but frequently neglected part of infrastructure management. You will not only learn the content, but also master it, thanks to the real-world activities and quizzes that pop up at regular intervals throughout the chapters.

Additionally, the book includes extensive coverage of best practices for scalability, environment isolation, and reusable modules. Finally, we get into how to integrate Terraform with other technologies, such as CDKTF, to provide you even more tools for infrastructure management.
Reading this book will open doors to exciting new opportunities in infrastructure management; it's about more than just picking up a tool. You will be well-prepared to become an expert in the field of Terraform after reading this book, which provides practical examples, real-world applications, and an easy-to-understand writing style. Thank you for joining me on this path of self-discovery.

Content

Preface

This all-inclusive book will take you from zero to hero in Terraform, a revolutionary tool from HashiCorp for managing and deploying datacenter infrastructure in the cloud or on-premises. Terraform is the key to unlocking the world of IaC. With the knowledge you gain from this book, you will be prepared to confidently take HashiCorp's Terraform Certification exam.

An extensive introduction to Terraform's architecture, covering its providers, resources, and state management features, sets the stage in the first chapter of the book. After you finish the first few chapters, you'll be behind the wheel, practicing for real-world situations with the help of several exercises. Using CloudOptic, a made-up but believable tech corporation, as an example, you will learn the ins and outs of module development and management. Starting with the basics and working its way up to advanced topics, this book walks you through every step of a Terraform project's lifetime.

Still, it's only the start. State manipulation commands, resource targeting, and handling configuration drifts are just a few of the tough but vital topics covered thoroughly in this book. With examples and practical suggestions provided, you will learn how to work with variables, output values, dependencies, and state files. This book will teach you all you need to know about reusable modules and more, so you can create and integrate your own.

The book's inclusion of exercises and real-world scenarios further increases its usefulness by providing ample opportunity to demonstrate mastery of the material. Every level of Terraform knowledge, from the most fundamental to the most complex, is covered thoroughly, preparing you to face any problem that comes your way.

In this book you will learn how to:

- Understand the fundamentals, including providers, resources, and state files.
- An in-depth look at making reusable modules, dealing with dependencies, and using versioning.
- Applicable, real-world context learning through the made-up corporation CloudOptic.
- Acquire knowledge of commands for manipulating states, handling drifts, and version control.
- Gain a grasp of the most important metrics and best practices for scaling Terraform systems.
- Proficiency in maintaining the Terraform codebase for future versions and ensuring compatibility.
- Instructions for setting up a connection between Terraform and the CDKTF.

- Code in accordance with industry standards to make Terraform scripts more dependable and cleaner.
- Prep for HashiCorp's Terraform Certification with tough quizzes and exercises.

GitforGits

Prerequisites

Anyone with a basic understanding of HashiCorp Terraform and a background in cloud, IT operations, devops, or software development can apply for this certification. Prior knowledge of on-premise and cloud architectural is preferred although not mandatory.

Codes Usage

Are you in need of some helpful code examples to assist you in your programming and documentation? Look no further! Our book offers a wealth of supplemental material, including code examples and exercises.

Not only is this book here to aid you in getting your job done, but you have our permission to use the example code in your programs and documentation. However, please note that if you are reproducing a significant portion of the code, we do require you to contact us for permission.

But don't worry, using several chunks of code from this book in your program or answering a question by citing our book and quoting example code does not require permission. But if you do choose to give credit, an attribution typically includes the title, author, publisher, and ISBN. For example, "Hashicorp Terraform Associate Certification (Exam 003) by Kimiko Lee".

If you are unsure whether your intended use of the code examples falls under fair use or the permissions outlined above, please do not hesitate to reach out to us at support@gitforgits.com.

We are happy to assist and clarify any concerns.

Acknowledgement

I owe a tremendous debt of gratitude to GitforGits, for their unflagging enthusiasm and wise counsel throughout the entire process of writing this book. Their knowledge and careful editing helped make sure the piece was useful for people of all reading levels and comprehension skills. In addition, I'd like to thank everyone involved in the publishing process for their efforts in making this book a reality. Their efforts, from copyediting to advertising, made the project what it is today.

Finally, I'd like to express my gratitude to everyone who has shown me unconditional love and encouragement throughout my life. Their support was crucial to the completion of this book. I appreciate your help with this endeavour and your continued interest in my career.

Chapter 1: Infrastructure-as-Code and Terraform

What is Infrastructure as Code (IaC)?

The Pre-IaC Era

Before the dawn of IaC, managing IT infrastructures was an arduous task. Traditionally, system administrators were responsible for manually setting up and managing servers, databases, and networking configurations. Each setup was unique, often described in extensive documentation that was prone to human errors and difficult to replicate.

In the fictional company "CloudOptic Solutions," the system administrators faced an uphill battle as they juggled multiple environments (development, testing, and production) across different projects. A considerable amount of time was spent in maintaining configurations, ensuring security, and resolving ad-hoc issues. This approach was not only time-consuming but also introduced the risk of 'configuration drift,' where environments diverged over time, making it harder to manage and troubleshoot.

Emergence of IaC

The industry's need for agility and scale propelled the search for better methods. As organizations began embracing agile methodologies and DevOps practices, the demand for automation rose exponentially. IaC emerged as a solution to this need. IaC enables businesses to manage and provision IT infrastructure through code, the same way they manage application development. This shift transformed "CloudOptic Solutions" by introducing standardization, eliminating manual setup tasks, and enabling a DevOps culture that broke down silos between operations and development teams.

Current Prospects and Adaptability of IaC

Today, IaC is no longer a 'nice to have'; it's considered a fundamental practice, especially for organizations aiming to implement a DevOps culture. It integrates naturally with other DevOps practices, such as Continuous Integration and Continuous Deployment (CI/CD), providing a comprehensive framework for automating not just application development but also infrastructure management.

CloudOptic Solutions, in its journey to modernize its IT landscape, embraced IaC to not just support its current cloud-based infrastructure but also to future-proof its investments. With IaC, the company can now experiment with new technologies and platforms more easily, adapt to multi-cloud strategies, and enforce policy-based governance on their infrastructure.

New technologies such as container orchestration and microservices are also increasingly IaC-friendly. In addition, the growing ecosystem of IaC tools like Terraform, Ansible, and others offers the adaptability and flexibility needed for modern infrastructures.

As we delve deeper into Terraform, we'll see how it offers a specific implementation of IaC, enabling CloudOptic Solutions to reap all these benefits and more. The learnings around

CloudOptic Solutions serves as an illustrative case study to better understand the practical applications of Terraform in a real-world scenario. While theoretical knowledge is essential, practical applications deepen that understanding, providing insights that are crucial for exam preparation as well. We will continually refer to the case of CloudOptic Solutions to learn every possible dimension, component and functions of Terraform, aiding your certification journey. The next sections will provide an in-depth look into how Terraform fits into the IaC landscape, how it can benefit your organization, and how it can resolve challenges like those faced by CloudOptic Solutions.

Advantages of IaC

The benefits that IaC brings to the table have transformative effects on how organizations approach infrastructure management. Each advantage compliments others, creating a synergistic impact that offers much more than just simplified management. We will dive deeper into the advantages that IaC provides, using the context of our fictional company, CloudOptic Solutions, to illustrate real-world applications of these benefits.

Cost-Efficiency

For starters, IaC significantly reduces the cost of infrastructure management. In the pre-IaC days, CloudOptic Solutions had to maintain a team of system administrators who manually set up, configured, and monitored various services. With IaC, many of these processes are automated, reducing the need for manual oversight and thereby cutting operational costs. Automated configurations are less susceptible to errors, reducing the resources needed for troubleshooting and corrections.

Improved Collaboration

IaC fosters an environment where the lines between development and operations blur. Developers, who are usually closer to the business logic, can now get involved in what was traditionally an Ops-only domain. For CloudOptic Solutions, this has led to an integrated DevOps culture where everyone is responsible for the end-product, fostering a more cooperative and efficient environment.

Speed and Agility

In today's fast-paced world, the ability to quickly adapt to market changes is invaluable. IaC enables rapid provisioning and tearing down of infrastructure, which is critical for scaling operations or deploying updates. This agility is manifested at CloudOptic Solutions through their CI/CD pipeline, which now includes infrastructure provisioning as a part of the build process, significantly reducing the time-to-market.

Consistency and Standardization

CloudOptic Solutions operates in a multi-cloud environment, making consistency a challenging goal. IaC offers the ability to reuse code snippets across various setups, ensuring that every environment is provisioned to the same specifications. This standardization eliminates the variability that often leads to bugs or security vulnerabilities, as every server, database, or other service is instantiated based on the same set of rules.

Version Control for Infrastructure

One of the game-changing advantages of IaC is the ability to apply version control to infrastructure the same way it is applied to software code. This has profound implications for tracking changes, rolling back to previous configurations, and auditing. For CloudOptic Solutions, any change made to the infrastructure can be reviewed, approved, or reversed, offering an audit trail and an additional layer of security.

Improved Disaster Recovery

Before IaC, disaster recovery was a highly stressful exercise that required significant manpower and hours of downtime. Now, your entire infrastructure, just like your codebase, can be version-controlled. CloudOptic Solutions maintains their infrastructure code in version-controlled repositories. In the event of a failure or a disaster, the infrastructure can be spun up again in a matter of minutes with the latest approved version, drastically reducing downtime and potential data loss.

Enhanced Security and Compliance

IaC allows organizations like CloudOptic Solutions to integrate security best practices into the code itself. This proactive approach is far more efficient than retroactively applying security patches. IaC also facilitates compliance management by allowing organizations to automate compliance policies directly into the code. This automated, code-based compliance significantly reduces the possibility of human error leading to security vulnerabilities.

Reusability and Modularity

Code written for infrastructure can be modular and reusable, just like software libraries. For instance, CloudOptic Solutions has different products requiring distinct configurations. However, many modules like logging, monitoring, and alerting are common across them. These modules are written once and reused across different products, saving time and effort.

Documentation and Knowledge Sharing

The code serves as the documentation in an IaC environment. This is invaluable for new team members who can understand the infrastructure setup by reviewing the codebase. At CloudOptic Solutions, this has dramatically reduced the onboarding time for new hires and facilitated knowledge sharing among team members.

Monitoring and Analytics

By codifying infrastructure, IaC enables better monitoring and analytics. The state of the infrastructure can be queried like a database. CloudOptic Solutions uses this capability to generate real-time reports on resource usage, cost management, and to make data-driven decisions for optimizing their services.

All things considered, IaC provides a simplified, cost-effective, and dependable method of infrastructure management, in addition to its many other benefits. It has far-reaching strategic benefits that influence many areas of company operations.

IaC Landscape

IaC has become an essential part of contemporary IT operations in today's dynamic digital world. However, the vastness and influence of IaC can only be grasped by delving into its ecosystem, which consists of the many tools, technologies, techniques, and best practices that make up IaC. In further sections and chapters, we will examine the larger IaC scene via the prism of CloudOptic Solutions.

Categories of IaC Tools

IaC tools can generally be classified into two broad categories:

Configuration Management Tools

These are primarily aimed at automating the setup, configuration, and management of servers. Examples include Puppet, Chef, and Ansible. CloudOptic Solutions initially employed Ansible to manage application configurations across its servers, before deciding to integrate IaC more extensively.

Orchestration Tools

These go a step further to manage the entire lifecycle of a service, from provisioning to maintenance to teardown. Terraform, AWS CloudFormation, and Azure Resource Manager (ARM) are examples. CloudOptic Solutions eventually shifted to Terraform due to its provider-agnostic nature, enabling them to manage multiple cloud providers through a single platform.

Imperative vs Declarative Languages

Imperative Languages

These focus on how to achieve a desired end state. Scripts in imperative languages spell out every step that needs to be executed. Although this allows for high flexibility, it often results in longer, more complex code.

Declarative Languages

These focus on what the end state should look like, without describing how to get there. Terraform's HashiCorp Configuration Language (HCL) is an example of a declarative language. For CloudOptic Solutions, switching to a declarative approach simplified the codebase and reduced the likelihood of errors.

Multi-Cloud and Hybrid Cloud IaC

One of the most notable trends in the IaC landscape is the move toward multi-cloud and hybrid cloud solutions. Companies like CloudOptic Solutions often rely on different cloud providers for various aspects of their business. IaC tools that are provider-agnostic, like Terraform, facilitate this by allowing organizations to manage multiple cloud services through a unified codebase.

IaC and Containers

The rising popularity of containerization technologies like Docker and Kubernetes has had a significant impact on the IaC landscape. These technologies allow for the encapsulation of applications in containers, which can then be managed through IaC scripts. CloudOptic Solutions, for example, uses Docker for containerization and Kubernetes for orchestration, both integrated into their IaC practices.

Code Repositories and Version Control

Git-based code repositories have become standard for storing IaC scripts. Version control platforms like GitHub, GitLab, and Bitbucket facilitate team collaboration, version tracking, and integration with CI/CD pipelines. CloudOptic Solutions maintains its IaC scripts in a Git repository that integrates with their Jenkins-based CI/CD pipeline.

IaC Security Tools

The IaC landscape also includes specialized security tools such as Checkov, KICS, and Terrascan, which scan IaC scripts for security vulnerabilities. As part of its comprehensive security strategy, CloudOptic Solutions integrates these tools into its CI/CD pipeline to automatically scan each update for security risks.

Infrastructure Monitoring and Telemetry

Monitoring solutions like Prometheus, Grafana, and Datadog are becoming increasingly integrated into the IaC landscape. These tools provide real-time insights into performance metrics, aiding in efficient resource management. CloudOptic Solutions employs Grafana dashboards to visualize the telemetry data from its various services, offering the team a consolidated view of system health.

Policy as Code

Policy as Code is a natural extension of IaC, allowing organizations to define and enforce security policies and compliance requirements as code. Tools like HashiCorp's Sentinel and Open Policy Agent enable this. CloudOptic Solutions uses Sentinel to enforce policies like least privilege access and data encryption across their Terraform-managed infrastructure.

IaC in CI/CD Pipelines

The integration of IaC into Continuous Integration and Continuous Deployment (CI/CD) pipelines is increasingly becoming a best practice. This approach allows organizations to automate not only code testing and deployment but also the provisioning and configuration of the underlying infrastructure. For CloudOptic Solutions, this has led to a fully automated deployment pipeline, significantly reducing manual interventions and associated risks.

The landscape of IaC is rich with community contributions and open-source projects. From modules in the Terraform Registry to Ansible Playbooks shared on GitHub, community contributions continually enrich the IaC ecosystem, providing organizations like CloudOptic Solutions with pre-built solutions and best practices that can accelerate their IaC adoption.

Terraform in IaC Ecosystem

As we dive deeper into the IaC landscape, particularly through the lens of CloudOptic Solutions, it becomes vital to examine one of the most influential and versatile tool viz, Terraform. Built by HashiCorp, Terraform has significantly impacted how companies like CloudOptic Solutions approach IaC. It's an orchestration tool that operates on a declarative model, using its domain-specific language called HashiCorp Configuration Language (HCL).

Provider-Agnostic Nature

One of the most compelling features of Terraform is its provider-agnostic nature. While many IaC tools are tied to specific cloud providers, Terraform is not. It offers "providers" that act as bridges to different platforms, including AWS, Azure, and GCP. This has proven to be a key decision driver for CloudOptic Solutions, which relies on a multi-cloud strategy for operational resiliency and efficiency. By employing Terraform, the company has been able to manage different cloud environments through a unified IaC framework.

Terraform's State Management

State management is another area where Terraform excels. It maintains a state file that reflects the real-time status of the resources it manages. This is a powerful feature, as it allows for performance optimizations and precise control over infrastructure changes. CloudOptic Solutions utilizes this feature to track the state of their cloud resources actively. It helps them in maintaining a history of configurations and modifications, enabling easy rollbacks if needed.

Modular Design and Reusability

Terraform promotes modularity and reusability through its design. Terraform modules are reusable, shareable, and configurable components that allow organizations to define and package IaC. This enables teams to build on the efforts of the broader community, saving time and improving code quality. For example, CloudOptic Solutions often relies on modules from the Terraform Registry, both to accelerate their projects and to implement best practices that have been community-vetted.

Policy as Code

While we learned Policy as Code in the broader landscape of IaC, it's worth noting that Terraform integrates natively with HashiCorp's Sentinel. Sentinel allows for policy as code practices, enabling organizations like CloudOptic Solutions to enforce company-wide policies automatically. This is not just a convenience but often a requirement in regulated industries, where compliance needs to be ensured across multiple layers of the stack.

Integration with CI/CD Pipelines

As in the case of CloudOptic Solutions, the integration of Terraform into Continuous Integration and Continuous Deployment (CI/CD) pipelines brings automation to another level. The terraform plan and terraform apply commands can be included as steps in the pipeline, ensuring that infrastructure provisioning is carried out automatically whenever new code is merged. This sort of automation is what enables CloudOptic Solutions to maintain agile, efficient, and reliable operations.

Collaboration and Workspaces

Terraform also offers features for enhanced collaboration. Workspaces, which are isolated environments to manage Terraform configurations, allow teams to collaborate without affecting each other's resources. This is particularly beneficial in a multi-cloud setting, as it permits separate teams at CloudOptic Solutions to work on AWS, Azure, or GCP projects without collision or overlap.

Extensibility and Custom Providers

Another defining characteristic of Terraform is its extensibility. While there are pre-defined providers for many platforms, it is also possible to write custom providers using Go. CloudOptic Solutions leveraged this to build custom integrations for their internal tools, turning ad-hoc scripts and APIs into manageable, version-controlled IaC components.

Drift Management

Terraform provides an efficient way to manage "drift" — the deviation of actual infrastructure from its desired state. Using commands like terraform refresh, CloudOptic Solutions can synchronize their local state file with real-world infrastructure, making it easier to understand and manage changes.

Key Concepts and Terminologies

Building on what we've learned from the case of CloudOptic Solutions, we will dive into the essential terms and concepts of Terraform, particularly useful for those who are just starting their journey into the cloud domain.

Terraform Configuration

Terraform uses a declarative language called HashiCorp Configuration Language (HCL) to describe the desired end-state of your infrastructure. You write this desired state in files with a .tf extension. In these files, you define resources, variables, outputs, and other elements. If you recall, CloudOptic Solutions maintained such .tf files to manage their multi-cloud environment.

Providers

Terraform uses plugins called "providers" to interact with cloud services, like AWS, Azure, or GCP, and even other services like GitHub or Kubernetes. Each provider offers a suite of resources you can manage. For example, the AWS provider allows you to create EC2 instances, S3 buckets, etc. Providers are central to how CloudOptic Solutions managed their multi-cloud setup.

Resources

Resources are the most critical elements in a Terraform configuration. They represent infrastructure objects, like compute instances, storage buckets, or DNS settings, that you wish to create, modify, or manage. CloudOptic Solutions, for example, had resources that represented their AWS EC2 instances and Azure VMs.

Variables and Outputs

Variables are parameters that allow you to customize your Terraform configurations. You can provide different values to variables when running Terraform commands to adapt the configuration to different environments or setups. Outputs are used to extract information about the infrastructure, like IP addresses or generated IDs, which can be used in other configurations or for reference.

State File

As learned while exploring CloudOptic Solutions, the state file (terraform.tfstate) is a JSON-formatted file that represents the current state of the managed infrastructure. This file is crucial for Terraform to determine which real-world resources correspond to the resources in your configuration.

Backend

The backend in Terraform determines where the state files are stored and how operations are executed. Backends can be local (stored on your machine) or remote (like S3 or Azure Blob Storage). CloudOptic Solutions used remote backends with encryption for enhanced security.

Plan and Apply Phases

In Terraform, before making any changes to the infrastructure, you create an execution plan using the terraform plan command. This command shows you what changes will be made based on your configuration files. Once you review the plan, you execute it using the terraform apply command, which makes the actual changes to the infrastructure. This is a fundamental part of the Terraform workflow.

Terraform Modules

Modules in Terraform are self-contained packages of configurations that are managed as a group. Modules can be used to create reusable components, improve organization, and to treat pieces of infrastructure as a single entity. CloudOptic Solutions employed both custom and publicly available modules to streamline their operations.

Terraform Workspaces

Workspaces allow you to maintain separate instances of your state file, facilitating managing different environments (like staging and production) more comfortably. Within CloudOptic Solutions, workspaces were utilized for isolation between different projects and environments.

Terraform Cloud

Terraform Cloud is a service provided by HashiCorp that offers collaboration and governance features for Terraform. This was a vital part of CloudOptic Solutions' multi-cloud management. It offers remote state management, API-driven runs, policy as code through Sentinel, and many other features that enhance team collaboration.

Sentinel

As mentioned in the CloudOptic Solutions case, Sentinel is HashiCorp's Policy as Code framework. With Sentinel, you can define fine-grained, logic-based rules to govern the behavior of infrastructure changes, thus enhancing governance and compliance measures.

Terraform Import

The terraform import command allows you to import existing infrastructure into your Terraform state. This is particularly useful when you've manually created resources and wish to bring them under Terraform management, similar to some practices at CloudOptic Solutions.

Drift Management

Drift refers to the deviation of the real-world infrastructure from the configuration defined in the Terraform files. CloudOptic Solutions managed drift by frequently running commands like terraform refresh to update the state file.

Secret Management

Terraform enables the secure management of sensitive data like API keys and passwords. Secret values can be input as variables or managed through a remote backend with encryption, as was the case at CloudOptic Solutions.

Terraform CLI Commands

Terraform provides a Command-Line Interface (CLI) with a range of commands for various tasks like initializing a directory (terraform init), validating the configuration (terraform validate), formatting the code (terraform fmt), and destroying the infrastructure (terraform destroy).

If you are just starting out in the cloud sector and want to become certified using Terraform, it is crucial that you understand these terms and concepts. As you continue learning, you will be able to understand increasingly advanced features and functions with the help of these fundamental building blocks.

Setting up Terraform on Linux

Stepping up to the next critical milestone: installing Terraform in a Linux environment, is the next logical step after grasping IaC concepts and delving into the basic terms of Terraform. To help you get going, I have compiled the following detailed steps.

Update Your Package Manager

Before you download Terraform, it's good practice to update your system's package manager. On an Ubuntu machine, this can be accomplished with:

```
sudo apt update && sudo apt upgrade -y
```

Download Terraform

Navigate to the official Terraform download page and download the appropriate version for your Linux distribution. Alternatively, you can use wget to download it from the command line. For example, to download Terraform version 1.0.0:

```
wget https://releases.hashicorp.com/terraform/1.0.0/terraform_1.0.0_linux_amd64.zip
```

Unzip the Archive

Once downloaded, unzip the archive using the unzip command:

```
unzip terraform_1.0.0_linux_amd64.zip
```

If unzip is not installed, install it with sudo apt install unzip.

Move Binary to /usr/local/bin

After unzipping the archive, you'll find a file named terraform in your current directory. This is a binary file, and for easier access, it's beneficial to move it to /usr/local/bin:

```
sudo mv terraform /usr/local/bin/
```

Verify Installation

To ensure that Terraform has been installed correctly, run:

```
terraform --version
```

You should see the Terraform version number displayed, confirming that the installation was successful.

Configure Environmental Variables

If you wish to set environment variables, like the AWS access and secret keys, you can do so using the export command:

```
export AWS_ACCESS_KEY_ID="your-access-key-id"

export AWS_SECRET_ACCESS_KEY="your-secret-access-key"
```

Create a Workspace

Make a new directory where you can store your Terraform files:

```
mkdir my-terraform-workspace

cd my-terraform-workspace
```

Initialize the Workspace

Initialize your Terraform workspace, which will download the provider plugins and create the initial .tfstate files:

```
terraform init
```

Create a Simple Configuration File

Within your workspace, create a new .tf file. We will start by making a file that provisions an AWS S3 bucket. Open a text editor and input the following HCL code, then save it as main.tf:

```
provider "aws" {
 region = "us-east-1"
}


resource "aws_s3_bucket" "my_bucket" {
 bucket = "my-unique-bucket-name"
 acl = "private"
}
```

Run Terraform Plan

Before applying the configuration, it's good practice to run terraform plan to see the changes that will be made:

```
terraform plan
```

Apply the Configuration

If the plan looks good, apply it:

```
terraform apply
```

You'll be asked to confirm by typing yes. Once confirmed, Terraform will create the AWS S3 bucket.

You will be able to successfully install Terraform on your Linux system by adhering to these steps. Always keep in mind that this is merely the foundation upon which you can construct increasingly elaborate systems. The story of CloudOptic Solutions should be considered; like you, they began small but scaled their operations efficiently with the help of Terraform.

Summary

The first step on our long trip in this chapter was to learn about IaC. We covered its history, advantages, and the ways it has changed IT operations through the automation of once manual processes, improvement of teamwork, and reduction of human mistake. Thanks to these features, IaC has become an industry standard in contemporary DevOps.

After covering IaC in general, we dove more into Terraform's niche within the IaC ecosystem. Using its state management features, Terraform is able to version your infrastructure and maintain it across several clouds, unlike many of its competitors. The introduction of the CloudOptic Solutions example served to highlight the practicality of the solution and the fact that even smaller enterprises are making good use of Terraform for managing complicated cloud infrastructures.

Chapter after chapter guided you through the fundamental principles and terminology of Terraform, providing entry-level cloud professionals with the tools they need to become proficient users of the platform. A seamless transition to hands-on application was achieved by covering concepts such as providers, resources, state files, and HCL (HashiCorp Configuration Language).

To wrap up our lessons, we demonstrated how to install Terraform on a Linux system in a thorough and error-free manner. This encompassed all aspects, from configuring a basic AWS S3 bucket to updating the system package management. As we go into more difficult topics in the next chapters, these core abilities will be a solid basis.

Test Exercise

These questions and scenarios are designed to test your grasp of the concepts and procedures learned in this chapter. Each question targets a specific aspect, from the basic understanding of IaC and Terraform to the practical knowledge required for setting it up and using it effectively.

1. What is IaC?
   a. A cloud service offered by AWS
   b. Manual configuration of servers
   c. The management of infrastructure through configuration files
   c. A type of programming language

2. What is a key benefit of IaC?
    a. It increases the complexity of infrastructure setup
    b. It minimizes human error
    c. It prolongs development cycles
    c. It discourages collaboration
3. How does Terraform differ from other IaC tools?
    a. It is limited to AWS
    b. It is not provider-agnostic
    c. It does not maintain state
    c. It is multi-cloud and provider-agnostic
4. Why was CloudOptic Solutions discussed in the chapter?
    a. To showcase a failure story
    b. To emphasize real-world applicability of Terraform
    c. To sell a product
    c. None of the above
5. You've been asked to store environment-specific variables securely in Terraform. What would you use?
    a. Hardcode them in the main.tf file
    b. Use Terraform Cloud for sensitive data
    c. Share them over email
    c. Store them in a public GitHub repository
6. In which directory would you run the terraform init command?
    a. The root directory
    b. The directory containing your .tf files (Terraform workspace)
    c. Any directory
    c. The /usr/local/bin directory
7. What does terraform plan do?
    a. Applies the configuration immediately
    b. Shows a list of all available commands
    c. Provides an output of changes to be made
    c. Initializes a new Terraform workspace
8. You see an error while applying a Terraform configuration. What could you enable to get more detailed logs?
    a. Debug mode in the main.tf file
    b. Verbose logging via environmental variables
    c. Contact customer support
    c. Delete and recreate the configuration

9. What language does Terraform use for its configuration files?

   a. JSON
   b. YAML
   c. HCL (HashiCorp Configuration Language)
   c. Python

10. After applying a configuration, you want to destroy all Terraform-managed resources. What command would you use?

    a. terraform delete
    b. terraform remove
    c. terraform destroy
    c. terraform clean

CHAPTER 2: UNDERSTANDING TERRAFORM BASICS

Understanding Providers

Introduction

At the heart of the Terraform ecosystem is the idea of providers, which is introduced in this chapter. Terraform relies on providers to connect to the many services and APIs you want to use, such as AWS, Azure, GCP, or even GitHub. The AWS provider is the one that knows how to convert your HCL code into API requests that AWS can comprehend when you use Terraform to construct an AWS EC2 instance, for example. Different providers offer different kinds of resources; for instance, AWS provides aws_instance, aws_vpc, and other similar types of resources.

In Terraform, every provider is a plugin, but not every plugin is a provider. Is it difficult to understand? Simplify, please. The extensibility of Terraform is made possible by its plugin-based architecture. One sort of plugin is the provider, and its sole purpose is to communicate with the application programming interfaces (APIs) of various service providers. Provisioners are one kind of plugin; others, like installers, deal with things like program installation and file uploads. So, providers aren't all plugins, but they are a significant fraction.

In order to manage APIs and services, providers provide fundamental building pieces called resource types. On the other hand, modules are more like pre-configured sets of resources designed to complete more complicated jobs. As an example, a VPC module may encapsulate all of the necessary steps to set up a Virtual Private Cloud (VPC) on AWS, saving you the trouble of developing ten separate resource blocks. Not being providers themselves, modules rely on providers.

How Providers Work?

A provider's role extends well beyond that of an API translator. In addition to supporting various versions, they maintain the status of resources and take care of API authentication. Terraform init will download the provider plugins you need, among other things. Within the Terraform configuration directory, there is a hidden directory where these are kept. This will ensure that every of your Terraform projects can have their own set of provider plugins without any conflicts.

Version control

When dealing with providers, it is essential to use proper versioning. When a provider is updated, it can bring new features or alter current ones. If you want your projects to act consistently, you can tell Terraform which provider version to use. To ensure that all team members are using the same provider version, you can define it in your Terraform configuration file.

Cross-Provider Support

The capacity of Terraform to accommodate numerous providers in a single setup is its strongest suit. This shines in situations involving many clouds or hybrid architectures. You can use the same

Terraform configuration to manage resources on both AWS and Google Cloud, for instance. It will be easier to develop all-encompassing infrastructure solutions since each supplier would be in charge of its own set of resources.

Provider Credentials

A provider's credential management system for API access is an important component. Terraform offers multiple options for safe credential handling because hardcoding credentials is risky. Use provider-specific mechanisms, such as AWS's shared credential file, or environment variables.

Think about a business that follows our example of CloudOptic Solutions and employs a multi-cloud approach. Their compute resources might be housed on AWS, while their data analytics could be run on Google Cloud. With Terraform, CloudOptic can easily automate and grow its infrastructure by defining and managing resources across several cloud providers.

Plugin-Based Architecture

Now that we've covered the basics of Terraform, we will have a look at its one of the distinguishing features, its plugin-based architecture, which makes it easy to extend to accommodate a broad range of service providers and provisioners. Each provider or provisioner in this architecture is a standalone executable (often built in Go) that talks to the main Terraform process over a clearly defined RPC (Remote Procedure Call) interface.

Basics

When you run a Terraform command, Terraform creates a separate process for each plugin it needs, whether that is a provider or a provisioner. These plugins then maintain an open line of communication with the main Terraform process over an RPC connection. Through this communication channel, Terraform can invoke specific functions within the plugin, whether it's to create, read, update, or delete a resource.

How Plugins Are Loaded?

Whenever you run terraform init, Terraform scans your configuration files to identify which providers you're using. If the necessary plugins are not already downloaded, Terraform fetches them from its plugin registry and stores them in a hidden .terraform directory within your working folder. This way, each project can have its own set of plugins, making it easier to manage dependencies.

Plugin Types

Terraform plugins are primarily of two types:

Provider Plugins

These are the most common types of plugins. Each cloud provider, like AWS, Azure, or GCP, has its own provider plugin.

Provisioner Plugins

These are used to execute scripts on a local or remote machine as part of resource creation or destruction. For example, you might use a provisioner to initialize a VM or to clean up before destroying it.

Custom Plugins

The extensible nature of Terraform allows you to write custom plugins, especially when an off-the-shelf solution doesn't meet your specific needs. These custom plugins can be written in Go and follow the same RPC protocol that built-in plugins use. This way, you can integrate Terraform with in-house software or lesser-known APIs.

Dependency Resolution in Plugins

Terraform's plugin-based architecture also includes built-in dependency resolution. Terraform creates a graph of all your resources and their dependencies and uses this to determine the order in which resources should be created, updated, or destroyed. Each plugin can declare what its resources depend on, and Terraform will use this information to optimize the execution plan.

Security Implications

Because plugins run as separate processes and have the ability to execute code, it's crucial to be cautious about where you download plugins from. Always ensure to use trusted sources. Terraform's plugin verification mechanisms add an extra layer of security by checksumming downloaded plugins and verifying their signatures.

Version Management

Just like providers, plugins can have different versions with distinct features and bug fixes. Terraform allows you to specify which versions of a plugin you wish to use, thus giving you control and ensuring backward compatibility. Let us say they're deploying a complex environment that integrates AWS for storage, Azure for Machine Learning, and an in-house database. The plugin architecture of Terraform allows CloudOptic to manage these diverse components effortlessly. Each provider plugin handles the intricacies of its respective service, while custom plugins can be developed for unique, in-house solutions.

Debugging and Logs

Lastly, Terraform provides extensive logging options for debugging plugins. By setting specific environment variables, you can capture detailed logs that help you trace any issues with the plugins.

Writing Configuration Files for CloudOptic

Terraform projects revolve around configuration files. What you intend to construct, alter, or remove from the infrastructure is defined by them. These configuration files, often saved with a.tf extension, are written in Terraform's proprietary domain-specific language, HashiCorp Configuration Language (HCL).

In order to fully grasp CloudOptic, we will first grasp this crucial component.

What are Configuration Files?

A configuration file contains the code that specifies the resources you need. This is where you write down what types of servers, databases, load balancers, and other infrastructure components you want to create. The configuration file also helps you set the relationships between these resources, dictate their order of creation, and define input variables and output parameters.

Components of Configuration Files

- Provider Block: Specifies which providers like AWS, Azure, or a custom provider will be used.
- Resource Block: Declares the resources to be managed, such as instances, databases, or VPCs.
- Variable Block: Allows you to define variables that you can later populate either through the command line or external files.
- Output Block: Specifies the data that you'd like to extract from the resources you've created, such as an IP address or URL.
- Data Block: Allows you to source data from your providers, so you can use it in other parts of your configuration.

Sample Program: Writing a Configuration File

Imagine for a second that CloudOptic wants to launch an EC2 instance and an S3 bucket through Amazon Web Services (AWS). In our.tf configuration file, we would include the following essential components for this:

Provider

First, specify that AWS is your provider and set the region.

```
provider "aws" {
```

```
region = "us-west-2"
}
```

EC2 Resource

Next, define an EC2 instance.

```
resource "aws_instance" "cloudoptic_instance" {
 ami = "ami-0c55b159cbfafe1f0"
 instance_type = "t2.micro"
 tags = {
 Name = "CloudOptic-Instance"
 }
}
```

S3 Resource

Define an S3 bucket where CloudOptic can store files.

```
resource "aws_s3_bucket" "cloudoptic_bucket" {
 bucket = "cloudoptic-bucket"
 acl = "private"
 tags = {
 Environment = "Dev"
 }
}
```

Variables and Outputs

To make the configuration flexible, we will add some variables.

```
variable "region" {

 default = "us-west-2"

}
```

And to extract the public IP of the EC2 instance:

```
output "instance_public_ip" {

 value = aws_instance.cloudoptic_instance.public_ip

}
```

Complete Configuration

Combining all these elements, your complete configuration file for CloudOptic would look like:

```
provider "aws" {

 region = var.region

}



resource "aws_instance" "cloudoptic_instance" {

 ami = "ami-0c55b159cbfafe1f0"

 instance_type = "t2.micro"

 tags = {

 Name = "CloudOptic-Instance"
```

```
 }
}

resource "aws_s3_bucket" "cloudoptic_bucket" {
 bucket = "cloudoptic-bucket"
 acl = "private"
 tags = {
 Environment = "Dev"
 }
}

variable "region" {
 default = "us-west-2"
}

output "instance_public_ip" {
 value = aws_instance.cloudoptic_instance.public_ip
}
```

Everything that CloudOptic requires is contained in this configuration file. It describes an EC2 instance and an S3 bucket, announces the AWS provider, and includes variables and outputs for data retrieval and flexibility. Your command of Terraform has progressed significantly since you learned how to organize this file. To ensure you're ready to take on any infrastructure challenge, we'll cover more sophisticated topics in the following section.

Resource Blocks and Attributes

Resource blocks are one of the most crucial parts of a Terraform installation. Accurately defining your architecture is possible with an understanding of resource blocks. To design individualized solutions, you get to choose what gets added, changed, or removed. A well-written resource block makes the codebase understandable, which in turn helps teams comprehend the current infrastructure—an understanding that is critical for maintenance in the long run. You can scale your infrastructure efficiently if you master the properties of resource blocks. In order to make room for expansion, you can simply restructure the current resource blocks. You can create connections between resources by learning to define and call characteristics. If you already have a database set up in a virtual private cloud (VPC), you may use that VPC reference in the EC2 resource block to set up an instance of Amazon Elastic Compute Cloud (EC2) in the same VPC. To excel at IaC with Terraform, familiarity with them is essential as explained in the further sub-topics.

What Are Resource Blocks?

Resource blocks define the infrastructure pieces you intend to create, manage, or even remove. These can range from virtual machines and network interfaces to higher-level components like DNS records. Each resource block specifies a particular type of object you want to manage, its characteristics, and how Terraform should interact with the service provider to manage that object.

Structure of a Resource Block

A typical Terraform resource block has the following basic structure:

```
resource "<PROVIDER_TYPE>" "<NAME>" {

 <ARGUMENT> = <VALUE>

 ...

}
```

- Provider_Type: This represents the type of resource you intend to create, e.g., aws_instance for an AWS EC2 instance or google_compute_instance for a Google Cloud VM.
- Name: This is a locally unique identifier for this resource, used within this Terraform script to refer to this particular resource.

- Arguments: These are key-value pairs that define the properties and configurations for that resource.

Understanding Attributes

Attributes are the specific details regarding a resource that you either configure or compute. Configurable attributes are set using the arguments within the resource block, whereas computed attributes are the ones that you can extract from the created resource but can't directly set. For example, the public IP of a newly created AWS EC2 instance is a computed attribute.

Sample Program: Using Resource Blocks and Attributes

Assume that CloudOptic wants to establish a connection between an existing EC2 instance and a newly deployed AWS RDS instance.

```
resource "aws_db_instance" "cloudoptic_db" {

 allocated_storage = 20

 storage_type = "gp2"

 engine = "mysql"

 engine_version = "5.7"

 instance_class = "db.t2.micro"

 name = "cloudopticdb"

 username = "cloudoptic"

 password = "yourpassword"

 parameter_group_name = "default.mysql5.7"

 skip_final_snapshot = true

}


resource "aws_instance" "cloudoptic_instance" {
```

```
ami = "ami-0c55b159cbfafe1f0"

instance_type = "t2.micro"


tags = {

Name = "CloudOpticInstance"

}


vpc_security_group_ids = [aws_db_instance.cloudoptic_db.security_group_names]

}
```

In the above example, we define two resource blocks—one for an AWS RDS instance and another for an EC2 instance. The aws_db_instance resource block includes attributes like allocated_storage, engine, engine_version, and so on. These are the configurable attributes. We also link this RDS instance to our EC2 instance through the vpc_security_group_ids attribute, showcasing how one resource can refer to another.

To summarize, in order to utilize Terraform effectively, you must have an in-depth knowledge of resource blocks and attributes. You can tailor the definition of your infrastructure to meet your unique needs while maintaining full control over the process.

Variables and Outputs

Terraform Variables

Terraform variables are similar to configuration parameters in that they can be changed. By enabling you to abstract details that can differ across environments, they facilitate configuration management and understanding. When you have a setup you want to reuse or sensitive data that needs to be separated from the configuration files, variables are a lifesaver.

Declaration

You declare variables using the variable block:

```
variable "instance_type" {

 description = "The instance type for EC2 resources"

 default = "t2.micro"

}
```

Utilization

Once declared, you can use variables within your configuration files like so:

```
resource "aws_instance" "example" {

 instance_type = var.instance_type

}
```

In the above code snippet, var.instance_type refers to the variable we declared earlier, allowing us to make the EC2 instance type configurable.

Outputs in Terraform

Contrary to variables, Terraform outputs allow you to retrieve data about the infrastructure even after it has been built. Anything related to the resource might be included, such as its IP address or DNS name.

Declaration

You declare outputs using the output block:

```
output "instance_public_ip" {

 value = aws_instance.example.public_ip

}
```

Utilization

Once your Terraform configuration has been applied, you can retrieve this output by running terraform output instance_public_ip. This will return the public IP address of the aws_instance.example that was created.

Sample Program: Using Variables and Outputs

We will enhance CloudOptic to grasp real-world variables and outputs. After we construct the resources, we'll make their EC2 instance type and RDS storage size adjustable with variables and then print their public IP and DNS.

Variable Configuration

```
variable "ec2_instance_type" {

 description = "EC2 instance type"

 default = "t2.micro"

}


variable "rds_allocated_storage" {

 description = "Allocated storage for RDS instance in gigabytes"

 default = 20

}
```

Resource Configuration with Variables

```
resource "aws_db_instance" "cloudoptic_db" {

 allocated_storage = var.rds_allocated_storage

 // ... other configurations

}


resource "aws_instance" "cloudoptic_instance" {

 instance_type = var.ec2_instance_type
```

```
// ... other configurations
}
```

By using variables, we've made it easier to customize the infrastructure setup without altering the main configuration.

Output Configuration

```
output "rds_endpoint" {
 value = aws_db_instance.cloudoptic_db.endpoint
}


output "ec2_public_ip" {
 value = aws_instance.cloudoptic_instance.public_ip
}
```

After applying this configuration, you can use terraform output rds_endpoint and terraform output ec2_public_ip to get the database endpoint and EC2 public IP, respectively.

Benefits of Variables and Outputs

- Variables make your Terraform code more reusable and customizable.
- Outputs let you easily access crucial data about your infrastructure, which can be used in other configurations or for informational purposes.
- Variables can also be parameterized in command-line arguments or in a Terraform Cloud workspace, giving even more dynamic capabilities to your IaC configurations.
- Sensitive data like API keys can be passed as variables, ensuring they are not hardcoded into the configuration.
- Outputs from one Terraform project can be used as variables in another, allowing for more complex orchestration of resources.

To sum up, variables and outputs are not just optional extras but essential features for writing effective, reusable, and maintainable Terraform code. They bring a level of dynamism and flexibility that are crucial for any complex infrastructure setup.

Popular Terraform Commands

Terraform provides a range of commands for different stages of the infrastructure lifecycle. For professionals who work with Terraform, mastering these commands is essential for effective infrastructure management. These commands streamline everything from initializing configurations to executing changes to maintaining state.

terraform init

The terraform init command initializes your Terraform working directory, downloading any necessary provider plugins and setting up the backend for storing your state file. Before you run any other Terraform command, you need to run terraform init.

```
terraform init
```

terraform validate

It's a good practice to validate your Terraform configuration files to ensure they are syntactically correct and internally consistent. The terraform validate command does just that.

```
terraform validate
```

terraform plan

Before making any changes to your infrastructure, you can see what Terraform will do by using the terraform plan command. This command is crucial for understanding what actions Terraform will take on your behalf.

```
terraform plan
```

terraform apply

After reviewing the execution plan, you can proceed with the terraform apply command, which will create or update your infrastructure to match your configuration.

terraform apply

terraform destroy

When you no longer need your infrastructure, or you wish to recreate it from scratch, you can use the terraform destroy command.

```
terraform destroy
```

terraform state

The terraform state subcommands help you manage Terraform's state data, which is used to map real-world resources to your configuration. The terraform state list command, for example, shows you all the resources in the state file.

```
terraform state list
```

terraform import

The terraform import command is used to bring already-existing infrastructure under Terraform management.

```
terraform import aws_instance.my_instance i-0abcdef1234567890
```

terraform fmt

The terraform fmt command is used to rewrite Terraform configuration files in a canonical format and style. It helps in maintaining the readability and consistency of Terraform code.

```
terraform fmt
```

terraform workspace

Workspaces are used to manage multiple distinct sets of infrastructure resources. The terraform workspace command allows you to create, change, and delete workspaces.

```
terraform workspace new dev
```

```
terraform workspace select dev
```

terraform output

We've learned outputs before, and this command is how you retrieve those output values. This command is especially useful for scripts to retrieve output values from a Terraform state file.

```
terraform output <output_name>
```

Sample Program: Using Commands

Let us say you're working on a CloudOptic project. You would start by initializing your workspace:

```
terraform init
```

Validate the configuration to ensure there are no errors:

```
terraform validate
```

Create an execution plan to understand what resources will be created or modified:

```
terraform plan
```

Apply the changes:

```
terraform apply
```

List the state to check all the CloudOptic-related resources:

```
terraform state list
```

These commands are your go-to for handling IaC on a daily basis. You can build, modify, and maintain infrastructure in a controlled and predictable manner if you know them thoroughly.

Understanding Terraform State

Terraform state is a critical concept for anyone who aims to use Terraform effectively. The state is Terraform's internal representation of the real-world infrastructure that you're managing. It serves as the "source of truth" for Terraform, mapping your configuration files to the actual resources it manages. To dive deeper, we will learn the mechanics of Terraform state, the state file, and its contents.

Mechanics of Terraform State

Terraform maintains a state to store the properties and configuration settings of managed resources. When you issue a command like terraform apply, Terraform references the current state to understand which real-world resources correspond to the resources in your configuration. This is essential for reconciling the differences between the desired state (what you specify in your configuration files) and the current state (what actually exists in the infrastructure).

If you define an AWS EC2 instance in your configuration and run terraform apply, Terraform will create the instance and store its details like instance ID, availability zone, and other attributes in its state. This is crucial because the next time you run terraform apply, Terraform will check this state to determine if the EC2 instance still aligns with your configuration or if changes are necessary.

terraform.tfstate

The state information is usually stored in a file called terraform.tfstate within your working directory. This file is generated automatically after you run terraform apply for the first time. This is considered the "local backend" but you can also configure remote backends like S3 or Azure Blob Storage for better safety and versioning.

Given below is a simplified example of what a terraform.tfstate file might look like for an AWS EC2 instance:

```
{
 "version": 4,
 "terraform_version": "0.14.2",
 "serial": 3,
 "lineage": "xyz",
 "outputs": {},
 "resources": [
```

```
{
"mode": "managed",
"type": "aws_instance",
"name": "my_instance",
"provider": "provider[\"registry.terraform.io/hashicorp/aws\"]",
"instances": [
{
"schema_version": 0,
"attributes": {
"id": "i-0abcdef1234567890",
"instance_type": "t2.micro",
// more attributes here
},
// other metadata
}
]
}
]
}
```

Components of State File

The terraform.tfstate file contains a lot of crucial information:

- Resource Attributes: It stores the attributes of all the resources that are managed by Terraform. This includes resource IDs, computed values, and any other attributes that are relevant to the resource.
- Backend Information: If you're using a remote backend, the state file will include metadata related to it, though the actual state might be stored remotely.
- Provider Information: The state file contains information on which providers are being used, along with their configurations. This is crucial for Terraform to know how to interact with your infrastructure services.
- Output Values: Any outputs that you've defined in your Terraform configuration will also be stored in the state file, making it easy to query those outputs later on.
- Dependencies: The state file tracks dependencies between resources, ensuring the correct order of creation, updating, and deletion.
- Version and Metadata: The state file also keeps track of the version of Terraform that is being used, ensuring that state is only modified by compatible versions of Terraform.

Take CloudOptic, for example. A variety of cloud resources, such as databases, network settings, and virtual machines, might be managed by you. Once you've run terraform apply, your state file will contain all the information on these resources associated with CloudOptic, including their IDs, attributes, dependencies, and more.

The terraform.tfstate file will keep track of many details, like the ID, hostname, and network settings, when you create a virtual machine. When deciding to scale, modify, or decommission that virtual machine, this information is crucial. Before applying any modifications to a particular virtual machine, Terraform checks the state file to ensure it's accurate.

The state is the backbone of your configuration, connecting it to the actual world and giving all the data you need to manage intricate infrastructures. The state file is a crucial component of any Terraform workflow, whether you're utilizing AWS, Azure, Google Cloud, or specialist services such as CloudOptic.

Viewing and Modifying Terraform State

Despite Terraform's best efforts, there may be times when you need to access or even edit the state manually. For CloudOptic, these further topics will teach you how to accomplish exactly that.

Viewing Terraform State

Terraform Show

One of the easiest ways to view the Terraform state is through the terraform show command. This command prints out the resources in the state file in a human-readable form. You can run it like this:

```
terraform show
```

If you are using a remote backend for your state, Terraform will download the state file temporarily to display its content. The command will show the attributes of all the resources managed by Terraform, such as their IDs, properties, dependencies, and more. For instance, for CloudOptic, you might see details about virtual machines, their IPs, and firewall settings.

Another option to see just the state outputs (like URLs, usernames, or other queryable information) is:

```
terraform output
```

JSON Output

If you need to analyze the state programmatically or feed it into some automated system, you can view the state in JSON format.

```
terraform show -json
```

This will produce a JSON output containing all the details found in your .tfstate file, a capability that could be useful in custom reporting or compliance checks within CloudOptic.

State List

You can also list resources within a state file using the following command:

```
terraform state list
```

This command will list the resources in the state file. For instance, in our CloudOptic scenario, you might see a list of all CloudOptic-related resources that you're managing.

Modifying Terraform State

Sometimes, direct state manipulation becomes unavoidable, although it's often considered risky and should only be performed with a complete understanding of the consequences. A safer way to edit the state is to use Terraform's built-in state manipulation commands. These commands can move, remove, or import resources.

Moving Resources

Let us say you want to rename a resource in your configuration without destroying it. In the context of CloudOptic, perhaps you want to rename a particular CloudOptic Virtual Machine for better categorization.

```
terraform state mv 'cloudoptic_vm.old_name' 'cloudoptic_vm.new_name'
```

Removing Resources

If you manually deleted a resource but it's still in the state file, you can remove it using:

```
terraform state rm 'cloudoptic_vm.old_name'
```

Importing Resources

If you've manually created a resource in CloudOptic and want to bring it under Terraform management, you can import it into your state file.

```
terraform import cloudoptic_vm.new_resource_id new-resource-ID
```

Before you modify the state in any way, it's recommended to take a backup. By default, running terraform apply or terraform destroy will create a backup of your state file as terraform.tfstate.backup. For additional safety, you can manually create a copy of the terraform.tfstate file. If something goes wrong, you can restore the state from this backup. Just replace the current terraform.tfstate with the backup file and run terraform apply again.

Summary

All of this chapter has centered on learning the ins and outs of Terraform's state management. Exploring several ways to see the Terraform state was the starting point for the notion. Among the many approaches considered were the following: terraform show, which displays the whole state; terraform output, which displays only the outputs; and terraform state list, which displays all of the resources contained in the state file. You may learn more about your CloudOptic infrastructure and how Terraform is managing it using these commands.

Shifting gears from observation to manipulation, the chapter explored the rationale and process behind manually modifying Terraform's state. Although it is technically feasible to alter the.tfstate file manually, doing so is risky. An alternative approach was to make use of the built-in state manipulation capabilities provided by Terraform. These functions allow users to move resources, remove resources, and import unmanaged resources into Terraform. By using these instructions, you can manage CloudOptic resources more carefully, without causing widespread modifications or ruining any current infrastructure.

We also learned how important it is to back up and restore the Terraform state file before making any manual modifications, and we touched on the subject briefly. If you want to protect your infrastructure from inconsistencies or mistakes caused by unintentional changes, this is the policy for you. The ability to backup and restore states gives users of CloudOptic an additional degree of security and operational comfort.

Test Exercise

1. What is the purpose of the terraform state list command?
    a. To delete resources from the state
    b. To view all resources in the current state
    c. To move resources in the state
    d. To import existing infrastructure into the state
2. How can you view the Terraform state for your CloudOptic infrastructure?
    a. Using terraform show
    b. Manually opening the .tfstate file
    c. Both A and B
    d. Neither A nor B
3. What is the risk associated with manually editing the .tfstate file?
    a. No risk involved
    b. Risk of introducing inconsistencies or errors
    c. Risk of exposing secrets
    d. Both B and C
4. Which command should you use to move a resource within a state file?
    a. terraform state move
    b. terraform state mv
    c. terraform mv
    d. terraform state transfer
5. Before making manual changes to the state file, what should you do?
    a. Run terraform init

b. Take a backup
c. Delete the .tfstate.backup file
d. Run terraform validate

6. What is the main use of terraform import in state management?
   a. To export the current state
   b. To move resources within the state
   c. To import existing infrastructure into Terraform management
   d. To delete resources from the state
7. Which command allows you to remove a resource from the Terraform state?
   a. terraform state delete
   b. terraform remove
   c. terraform state rm
   d. terraform del
8. In the context of CloudOptic, why is backing up the state file crucial?
   a. To rollback to a previous state
   b. To replicate the state on another machine
   c. To guard against accidental alterations
   d. All of the above
9. Which command should you use to query only the output values from the state file?
   a. terraform state show
   b. terraform output
   c. terraform state output
   d. terraform show-output
10. What does the terraform state show [address] command do?
    a. Shows the state of all resources
    b. Shows the state of a specific resource defined by the address
    c. Deletes the specified resource from the state
    d. Moves the specific resource to another state

CHAPTER 3: TERRAFORM WORKFLOW

Terraform Workflow Overview

When it comes to managing cloud infrastructure, the Terraform workflow provides a strategy that is rigorous, predictable, and scalable. In its most basic form, it is a collection of instructions and procedures that are intended to provide cloud experts with complete control over their environment. Workflow consists of three primary phases: writing, planning, and creating and applying. Organizations are able to maximize their utilization of cloud resources, guarantee that they are in compliance with industry standards, and reduce the risks associated with their operations if they adhere to this approach.

Before diving into the components of the Terraform workflow, it's vital to understand the business and technological advantages that have led to positive customer experiences. Several companies, especially those in industries requiring high compliance, have lauded the transparency and auditability that come with Terraform's approach.

- Predictable Costs: Businesses have found that the Plan phase, where the effects of changes are previewed before application, helps them understand the cost implications, enabling better budget management.
- Reduced Error Rate: The Preview feature allows teams to catch errors before they go live. This proactive error detection results in fewer incidents, reducing the Mean Time To Repair (MTTR) and improving system reliability.
- Version Control: By treating IaC, companies can version their infrastructure the same way they do with software code. This versioning allows them to roll back to previous stable versions easily, making it extremely valuable in regulated industries.
- Speed of Deployment: For e-commerce platforms where scalability is key, the Terraform workflow provides rapid deployments. The Write-Plan-Apply cycle can be automated, and infrastructure can be spun up and torn down quickly, thus supporting agile development methodologies.
- Cloud Agnostic: One of the most compelling stories comes from businesses operating in a multi-cloud environment. Terraform stands out for its cloud-agnostic approach, allowing businesses to manage resources across different cloud providers seamlessly.

In our running example, CloudOptic leveraged Terraform to manage its multi-cloud strategy, consolidating cloud services into a unified workflow. This led to a 40% reduction in operational overhead, streamlining their DevOps cycles.

To summarize, the Terraform workflow is an embodiment of best practices in infrastructure management which we will explore in our next section. This workflow sits at the core of how Terraform operates, offering a standardized approach that can be scaled up or down depending on an organization's needs.

Terraform Workflow Phases

Starting from the last section, we will go further into the Terraform workflow's three stages: writing, planning, and creating/applying. The ability to use Terraform for infrastructure management efficiently depends on a thorough understanding of these stages.

Write Phase

In the Write Phase, you'll define the infrastructure you need in code using HashiCorp Configuration Language (HCL). HCL is designed to be both machine-readable and human-friendly, thus striking a balance between readability and automation capabilities.

Example

CloudOptic has been our working example throughout this whole thing, so we will think about it. Now we'll imagine CloudOptic is interested in establishing an Amazon Elastic Compute Cloud (EC2) connection. This is one possible representation of the HCL code:

```
provider "aws" {

 region = "us west 2"

}


resource "aws_instance" "example" {

 ami = "ami-0c55b159cbfafe1f0"

 instance_type = "t2.micro"


 tags = {

 Name = "CloudOptic-Example"

 }

}
```

In this code, we define a provider (aws) and specify its region. Then, we define a resource (aws_instance) that we want to create, specifying the type of Amazon Machine Image (AMI) and the instance type. Simple tags are also added for easier identification later.

Plan Phase

The Plan Phase is where you visualize the effects of your code before actually executing it. It performs a dry run to reveal what will be added, modified, or destroyed. This is crucial for validating the configuration, ensuring it's correct and safe to apply.

Example

Continuing with the CloudOptic scenario, executing terraform plan in the directory containing the above HCL code would output an execution plan. The plan shows you exactly what will happen when you apply this configuration. For instance, it may tell you that one new EC2 instance will be created.

```
Plan: 1 to add, 0 to change, 0 to destroy.
```

This output helps you confirm whether your changes align with your intended outcomes. It serves as a final check to avoid unwanted alterations to your environment.

Create/Apply Phase

Once you've reviewed and are satisfied with your plan, the next phase is the Create/Apply phase. Here, you'll execute the changes you previewed in the Plan Phase by running the terraform apply command. This action creates or modifies the resources as per the configuration.

Example

Continuing with CloudOptic, you would execute terraform apply after the plan has been validated. After you give Terraform another green light, it will show you the execution plan once again. After you provide the go-ahead, the AWS EC2 instance will be created.

```
aws_instance.example: Creating...

aws_instance.example: Still creating... [10s elapsed]

aws_instance.example: Creation complete after 15s [id=i-0c23456789abcdef0]
```

At this point, Terraform has successfully created the resource as per your configuration, and it's live on AWS. This hands-on execution ensures you know exactly what is happening at each stage, making the entire process transparent and controlled.

Initializing Terraform Directory

The next key step in the Terraform workflow is to initialize your Terraform working directory. The purpose of initialization is to prepare the directory that contains your Terraform configuration files (.tf files) for execution.

- This stage is particularly crucial for a few reasons:
- Terraform uses providers to interact with various cloud services. Initializing the directory downloads the necessary provider plugins you've specified in your configuration.
- The backend is responsible for storing your Terraform state. Initialization allows you to configure this, whether you're storing it locally or in a cloud storage service.
- If your configuration calls other modules, initialization will download and prepare these as well.
- It also validates the syntax of your configuration files, ensuring that they are correctly structured.

Create Terraform Configuration Files

Before initializing, ensure you have a Terraform configuration file (.tf) in your working directory.

We will assume you have an main.tf file with the following AWS EC2 instance configuration.

```
provider "aws" {

 region = "us-west-2"

}



resource "aws_instance" "cloudoptic_instance" {

 ami = "ami-0c55b159cbfafe1f0"

 instance_type = "t2.micro"



 tags = {
```

```
Name = "CloudOptic-Instance"
}
}
```

Open Terminal and Navigate to Directory

Open your terminal and navigate to the directory where your main.tf resides.

```
cd path/to/your/terraform/directory
```

Initialize the Directory

Run the terraform init command to initialize the directory.

```
terraform init
```

Expected Output

When you run this command, you should see output similar to the following:

```
Initializing the backend...


Initializing provider plugins...
- Finding latest version of hashicorp/aws...
- Installing hashicorp/aws v3.53.0...
- Installed hashicorp/aws v3.53.0 (signed by HashiCorp)


Terraform has been successfully initialized!
```

Troubleshooting Tips

- If you've specified a version for your provider that is not compatible with your Terraform version, you'll encounter an error. Do not forget to align the versions properly.
- Ensure you have a stable internet connection, as provider plugins need to be downloaded.
- Ensure you have the necessary permissions to write to the directory. Otherwise, initialization may fail due to access issues.

Initializing is more than a mere prerequisite; it's the foundational step that configures the environment in which you'll work. It's critical to know what happens during this stage and how to troubleshoot any issues that may arise, so your subsequent activities with Terraform go smoothly.

Validating Terraform Configuration

Once you've initialized your Terraform directory, the following step is to confirm your setup. When making modifications to your infrastructure, like in our current CloudOptic example, this often-overlooked but critical step in the Terraform workflow must be followed. You can check the syntax and internal consistency of your configuration files by running a validation test, which does not alter the files in any way.

To become an expert in this area, follow these steps:

What is Configuration Validation?

Configuration validation involves two key aspects:

Syntax Check

Validates that your .tf files are written correctly. Checks for things like missing brackets, commas, or any other syntax-related errors.

Attribute Check

Ensures that attributes and arguments you've defined for your resources are compatible with the chosen provider's schema.

How to Validate Configuration

Open Your Terminal

Navigate to your Terraform directory where your main.tf file is located (our ongoing CloudOptic example).

```
cd path/to/your/terraform/directory
```

Run the Validate Command

Run the following command to validate your configuration:

```
terraform validate
```

Expected Output

If all is well, you'll see:

```
Success! The configuration is valid.
```

If there are errors, the command output will provide details, guiding you on what to fix.

Tips for Validation

If you're using a specific version of a provider, validate against that.

As a best practice, validate the configuration after each modification.

Remember, terraform validate doesn't evaluate variables. It only checks that their declared types and given values are compatible.

Advanced Validation

While terraform validates checks for syntax and basic attribute compatibility, it doesn't cover every possible issue. Other measures include:

- Running terraform plan will give you a detailed outline of what changes Terraform intends to make, catching some issues that might not.
- For complex configurations, some users opt to write custom validation scripts to check for domain-specific rules or company policies.

By incorporating these principles into our CloudOptic example, we can make validation a regular part of our process rather than an afterthought. This guarantees that your code-based infrastructure is not only functional, but also strong and devoid of errors.

Execution Plan

The next critical step in the Terraform process, which is applicable to our current CloudOptic situation, is to create and comprehend the execution plan. You can think of the execution plan as a "preview" of the infrastructure modifications that Terraform will make. Your syntax will be guaranteed to be correct when you validate your settings. But it's equally important to know how your modifications will affect operations before you make them.

What is an Execution Plan?

An execution plan is an outline of what actions (add, update, destroy) Terraform will take to align your infrastructure with your configuration. It's essentially a "what will happen" report that helps you review changes before they are applied.

Importance of Execution Plan

- It serves as a safety measure, allowing you to verify what will happen when you run terraform apply.
- It provides a transparent view into how your actions will affect your existing resources, which is crucial for complex environments like CloudOptic.
- In regulated environments, or where changes involve multiple stakeholders, the execution plan can be reviewed and approved before implementation.

Step-By-Step Execution Plan

Navigate to Terraform Directory

As in the validation stage, open your terminal and navigate to the directory where your CloudOptic Terraform configuration resides.

```
cd path/to/your/terraform/directory
```

Run terraform plan

Now, create the execution plan by running:

```
terraform plan
```

Review the Plan

The output will categorize changes as:

- \+ create
- \- destroy

- ~ update in-place
- -/+ destroy and then create
- ± create or destroy, depending on some conditions

Each section will detail the exact changes to the attributes of the resources.

Check Dependencies

The execution plan also respects dependencies between resources, so changes are made in the correct order. For example, if a subnet depends on a VPC, Terraform won't attempt to create the subnet until the VPC is up.

Additional Flags and Options

- Output to File: To save the plan to a file, use the -out flag like so:

```
terraform plan -out=myplan.tfplan
```

- Variable Values: You can include variable values in the plan:

```
terraform plan -var="image_id=ami-abc123"
```

- Targeted Resources: You can target specific resources:

```
terraform plan -target=aws_instance.my_instance
```

- Refreshing State: By default, terraform plan performs a refresh. To skip the refresh:

```
terraform plan -refresh=false
```

What to Look For?

- Are there any resources being modified or destroyed that you didn't intend to change?
- Are the attribute values what you expect?
- Are resources being created in the logical order respecting dependencies?

You may significantly improve your ability to manage your CloudOptic infrastructure if you familiarize yourself with the execution plan and use it on a regular basis. The additional security and predictability it provides is significantly appreciated in the dynamic world of IaC.

Applying Changes with Terraform

The following sensible step, after thoroughly reviewing your execution plan, is to implement the changes you have intended to make to CloudOptic's infrastructure. When you apply changes in Terraform, your execution plan is put into action and your configuration is brought into alignment with your real-world infrastructure, which could be the creation, modification, or destruction of resources. This step makes the state of your infrastructure congruent with what is described in your Terraform configuration files.

Importance of Applying Changes

- Manifestation of Configurations: This is the stage where your code becomes a reality. Your CloudOptic infrastructure will actually be updated according to your plan.
- Resource Allocation: Resources like virtual machines, databases, and networks are provisioned or adjusted.
- State Update: After successfully applying changes, Terraform updates the state file to reflect the new state of the infrastructure.

Step-By-Step To Apply Changes

Initiate Apply Command

Navigate to the directory containing your CloudOptic configuration, if you aren't already there, and run:

```
terraform apply
```

Review and Approve

Terraform will once again generate an execution plan and ask for your approval. This is your last chance to ensure that you're comfortable with the changes.

You'll need to type yes to proceed. This is a built-in safety feature to prevent accidental changes.

Monitor the Output

As Terraform proceeds, it will display the resources it's creating, modifying, or destroying. Watch this output carefully for any errors or issues. If everything goes smoothly, you should see a message indicating that the changes were applied successfully.

Validate in CloudOptic

To be very sure, manually verify that the desired changes have been implemented in your CloudOptic environment.

State File Update

Check the updated terraform.tfstate file, which will now represent the new, current state of your CloudOptic resources. You can either view it in your text editor or by running terraform show.

Additional Commands and Flags

To skip the manual approval, use the -auto-approve flag. This is useful for automated pipelines but use cautiously.

```
terraform apply -auto-approve
```

If you only want to apply changes to specific resources:

```
terraform apply -target=aws_instance.my_instance
```

To limit the number of concurrent operations as Terraform walks your graph:

```
terraform apply -parallelism=5
```

Just like in the plan phase, you can pass variables during apply:

```
terraform apply -var="image_id=ami-abc123"
```

If you saved your plan to a file:

```
terraform apply "myplan.tfplan"
```

To become an expert at turning your setups into real-world scenarios, particularly in your CloudOptic environment, you need to master the 'apply' stage. The "rubber meets the road" at this point, and the resources you saw in your code now exist in the real world.

Handling Unintended Changes

In the CloudOptic environment you're working with, knowing how to handle unforeseen changes is a must when using Terraform for infrastructure management. Unintended consequences, such as the loss or damage to resources, can result from these modifications. A poorly built execution plan, configuration drift, or human mistake are among the many potential causes of unexpected changes. You must be aware of the causes and ways to prevent these problems.

How Unintended Changes Occur?

Configuration Drift

Configuration drift refers to the divergence of the actual state of the infrastructure from its desired state as defined in your Terraform files. Drift could happen due to manual changes made directly to the CloudOptic platform or by some automated process that isn't managed through Terraform.

Human Error

A simple typographical mistake, incorrect variable, or even a misplaced bracket can cause your configuration to behave unexpectedly. If not caught during the review of the execution plan, these can lead to unintended consequences.

Versioning Issues

Outdated or incompatible versions of providers, modules, or even Terraform itself can introduce inconsistencies. This is especially true if you're working in a team environment where different team members might use different versions.

Interdependencies

Resources in CloudOptic, and in cloud platforms in general, can be interdependent. Unintended changes can ripple through these dependencies if not properly accounted for.

Consequences of Unintended Changes

- The most feared unintended change is resource destruction. Accidentally deleting a critical database or storage volume in CloudOptic can have catastrophic implications.
- Creating resources that are not needed can result in unnecessary costs. Similarly, deleting resources can also trigger financial penalties, particularly if you're dealing with reserved instances.
- Unintended changes can open security loopholes. For instance, a misconfigured network ACL or security group can expose your CloudOptic infrastructure to unwanted traffic.

How to Minimize the Risk of Unintended Changes?

Thoroughly Review Execution Plan

Always review the execution plan generated by the terraform plan command before applying changes. The plan outlines what Terraform intends to do, which can help you spot errors or omissions that could lead to unintended changes.

Use terraform destroy Wisely

This command is a double-edged sword. It can clean up resources but can also destroy vital components if not used carefully. Always review the resources listed for destruction and ensure that they are the ones you actually intend to destroy.

Test Environments

Before deploying changes to your production CloudOptic environment, test the changes in a separate staging environment that mimics your production setup as closely as possible.

Version Control

Keep your Terraform configurations in a version control system like Git. This allows you to track changes over time, making it easier to identify what may have gone wrong if unintended changes occur.

Backups and Snapshots

For critical resources like databases, always have backups or snapshots available. If something goes wrong during a Terraform apply operation, you can quickly restore your CloudOptic environment to its previous state.

Policy as Code

Tools like HashiCorp's Sentinel can enforce policies, providing another layer of protection against unintended changes. You can define what is and is not permissible, thereby reducing the risk of accidental destruction or modification.

Limit Permissions

Implement least-privilege access controls in CloudOptic and your Terraform setup. This limits the scope of what can be changed, reducing the risk of unintended changes occurring in the first place.

Locking State Files

State files can be locked to prevent simultaneous operations that might lead to conflicts and unintended changes.

You can better take precautions against unforeseen developments if you are aware of their potential entry points. You may significantly reduce the likelihood of unanticipated changes or loss of resources in your CloudOptic environment by implementing safeguards, routinely evaluating execution plans, and making use of extra tools.

Formatting and Style in Terraform

The logic you're implementing is important, but so is maintaining consistency in the style and formatting of your code. Misunderstandings, mistakes, and collaboration issues might result from code that is inconsistent or poorly formatted. You can keep your formatting and style consistent with the built-in tools and guidelines provided by Terraform. Terraform fmt is one such utility; it updates Terraform configurations automatically so they follow a consistent style and structure.

Terraform Formatting and Style Guidelines

Indentation

Terraform recommends two spaces for indentation. This keeps the codebase readable without taking up unnecessary horizontal space.

```
resource "cloudoptic_instance" "example" {

 name = "example-instance"

 type = "t2.micro"

}
```

Attribute Naming

In Terraform, the attribute names should be in snake_case. For example, instance_type is preferred over InstanceType or instance-type.

Resource Naming

Resource names within the configuration should also be snake_case and descriptive enough to understand the purpose but not so verbose that they become cumbersome.

```
# Good

resource "cloudoptic_network_security_group" "web_sg" {}
```

Bad

resource "cloudoptic_network_security_group" "SecurityGroupForWebServers" {}

Comments and Documentation

Inline comments should start with a # followed by a space. Block comments, though rarely used in Terraform, follow the /* ... */ syntax. Comments should be used to describe why something is done a certain way, not what is being done, which should be self-evident from the code.

Good Practice

Enable monitoring for the web instance

monitoring = true

Bad Practice

Setting monitoring to true

monitoring = true

File Structure

Terraform configurations can span multiple files. It's good practice to separate resources into different files and folders based on their purpose or function. For example, all CloudOptic network-related resources could be in a network.tf file.

Terraform fmt Command

One of the most beneficial features Terraform offers for code formatting is the terraform fmt command. This command automatically rewrites Terraform configuration files to a canonical format and style, thus ensuring that the codebase remains consistent.

What Does terraform fmt Do?

- It aligns the equals signs (=) in the argument declarations.
- It indents blocks of nested arguments consistently.
- It ensures a single empty line between resource blocks for readability.

Running this command within your working directory restructures your Terraform files according to the established guidelines. This is particularly useful in team environments where multiple people might be working on the same Terraform configuration.

Usage Example

Consider the following unformatted Terraform configuration for CloudOptic:

```
resource "cloudoptic_instance" "example"{name="example-instance" type="t2.micro"}
```

Running terraform fmt would transform this to:

```
resource "cloudoptic_instance" "example" {

 name = "example-instance"

 type = "t2.micro"

}
```

Verbose Logging

One way to debug or keep tabs on how an application is behaving is with verbose logging, which provides extensive information about activities and transactions. The complex complexities of resource provisioning, state management, and API interactions can be better understood with verbose logging.

Verbose logging serves multiple purposes:

- Helps in identifying issues during development.
- Offers detailed event tracking for audit purposes.
- Provides insights into performance bottlenecks.

How to Enable Verbose Logging in Terraform?

Terraform uses an environment variable named TF_LOG to manage log levels. The variable can take values such as TRACE, DEBUG, INFO, WARN, and ERROR. To enable verbose logging, set this environment variable to a higher log level like DEBUG or TRACE.

Enabling Verbose Logging

On a Linux system, you can enable verbose logging by running:

```
export TF_LOG=DEBUG
```

Or, for even more detail:

```
export TF_LOG=TRACE
```

After setting this variable, subsequent terraform commands will produce detailed logs.

Output Log File

Terraform also allows you to save logs to a file for persistent storage using the TF_LOG_PATH environment variable:

```
export TF_LOG_PATH=./terraform.log
```

Verbose Logging in CloudOptic with Terraform

To understand verbose logging specific to CloudOptic, you would generally look for API interactions and resource provisioning details in the log.

The logs will show the RESTful API calls made to CloudOptic. You can see the request and response headers, body, and status codes. This is valuable for debugging authentication issues, understanding rate limiting, or seeing what data CloudOptic is returning.

```
2022-05-12T15:34:22.125 [DEBUG] plugin.terraform-provider-cloudoptic: 2022/05/12 15:34:22 [DEBUG] CloudOptic API Request Details:

---[ REQUEST ]---------------------------------------

GET /api/v1/resource HTTP/1.1
```

When Terraform creates, updates, or destroys a resource in CloudOptic, those operations will be shown in detail in the logs.

```
2022-05-12T15:34:22.528 [DEBUG] apply: cloudoptic_instance.example: Creating...
```

Logs will also reveal how Terraform is managing the state file during operations. Any locking or unlocking of state files, and state versioning will be shown.

```
2022-05-12T15:34:23.729 [DEBUG] state: Acquiring lock for state file
```

For performance analysis, the logs will show how much time individual operations are taking.

```
2022-05-12T15:34:24.000 [DEBUG] cloudoptic_instance.example: Creation complete after 2s
```

Any issues or warnings during the apply phase will be detailed, providing insights into what went wrong.

```
2022-05-12T15:34:25.410 [WARN] Invalid value for attribute
```

Let us say you are dealing with a seemingly inexplicable error while trying to create a new instance. Enabling verbose logging can expose under-the-hood problems such as invalid parameters or insufficient permissions.

You would activate verbose logging with the export TF_LOG=DEBUG command and then rerun your terraform apply. The logs would then show if the API call to CloudOptic failed due to some invalid data, allowing you to pinpoint the issue's source more efficiently.

Summary

We covered a lot of ground in this chapter about Terraform workflows, including its many parts, with an emphasis on writing, planning, and building. We delved into the practicality of initialization and how it facilitates a seamless deployment by laying the groundwork for subsequent actions. Terraform has many in-built techniques to check configurations before running them, which helps to minimize errors and possible downtime. We next dove into the execution plans, which lay out the groundwork for Terraform's actions and provide one last chance for review before implementing infrastructure changes.

We discovered the importance of the state file in keeping your infrastructure's resources in their current state as we moved into managing Terraform state. In order to optimize and verify your configuration, Terraform uses this file to map real-world resources to it. Modifying and visualizing the Terraform state is essential for troubleshooting and resource management, and we addressed that and more in our practical state management section.

We also dedicated a lot of time to going over the extensive logging that Terraform offers for monitoring and debugging. This required extensive familiarity with the various log formats, their respective implementations, and their interpretation, with a focus on CloudOptic. Not only does verbose logging help with debugging, but it's also significantfor audits and compliance. By demonstrating Terraform's interaction with the CloudOptic API using CloudOptic-specific verbose logging examples, we were able to gain a deeper understanding of resource provisioning, state management, and error handling.

We introduced the terraform fmt command, which updates configurations to a standard format automatically, and learned about the importance of formatting and style in the area of code quality. We next looked at the idea of unforeseen changes, such as the destruction of infrastructure, which highlighted the importance of thorough planning and validation in order to prevent the unintentional depletion of resources. All of these parts work together to make up a Terraform practitioner's day, and they give the tools for good infrastructure management.

Test Exercise

1. What is the first phase of the Terraform workflow?
    a. Plan
    b. Create
    c. Write
    d. Initialize
2. Which command initializes a new or existing Terraform configuration?
    a. terraform plan
    b. terraform init
    c. terraform validate
    d. terraform apply
3. What is the purpose of terraform validate?
    a. To apply changes to the infrastructure
    b. To initialize the directory
    c. To check for syntactical correctness
    d. To create an execution plan
4. What does the Terraform state file store?
    a. The IP address of the server
    b. The API keys used
    c. The current state of resources

   d. The desired state of resources

5. Which Terraform command helps to format the configuration files?
   a. terraform format
   b. terraform style
   c. terraform fmt
   d. terraform refactor
6. In the CloudOptic environment, what does verbose logging help with?
   a. Increasing CPU usage
   b. Debugging and auditing
   c. Internet connectivity
   d. Load balancing
7. Which phase of the Terraform workflow allows you to review changes before they are applied?
   a. Write
   b. Initialize
   c. Plan
   d. Validate
8. What is the risk of skipping the planning phase in Terraform?
   a. Syntax errors
   b. Resource leaks
   c. Unintended changes, like destroying infrastructure
   d. Running out of disk space
9. In which phase are resources actually provisioned in the Terraform workflow?
   a. Plan
   b. Create
   c. Write
   d. Validate
10. If you want to inspect the details of the Terraform operation and interactions with CloudOptic API, which log level should you use?
   a. INFO
   b. DEBUG

c. WARN
d. ERROR

Chapter 4: State Management and Backend

Introduction to Terraform Backend

The concept of a "backend" in Terraform has significance in the world of IaC, particularly for managing the state files. The previous chapters covered the groundwork, but now we'll move on to the backends. Here, we'll be concentrating on the local backend in particular.

The execution of operations like apply and the loading of the state are both controlled by a Terraform backend. Because it records the metadata and configurations applied to your infrastructure's resources, the state is vital. Each of the many potential backends has its own set of advantages and disadvantages. The local backend keeps the state file locally on your PC, as the name implies. For the most part, this works well for practice or smaller projects.

Local Backend

When you execute Terraform commands like init, apply, or destroy, these commands interact with the backend. The local backend writes and retrieves state data from a file on your local filesystem. This is the default backend and doesn't require any additional configuration to set up. The state file, named terraform.tfstate, is JSON-formatted and includes all the details about the resources you're managing.

Storage and Security Concerns

Storing the state file locally can raise concerns regarding data security and collaboration. Because the state file can contain sensitive data, storing it on a local machine can expose you to risks. This storage method also has limitations when it comes to team collaboration. When multiple team members are working on the same project, using local backends may result in conflicts. This is why other backend types like S3 or Azure Blob Storage are often preferred for larger projects.

How it Works?

For smaller installations or test scenarios in a CloudOptic environment, using a local backend could be a good starting point. You can begin by performing plan and apply operations after initializing your Terraform configurations for CloudOptic resources. Here, you'll be running these tasks from the same system where the state file is located. Nevertheless, you could wish to upgrade to more powerful backend technologies, such as AWS S3, that CloudOptic is compatible with, when your infrastructure expands.

Suppose you're managing a few virtual machines and some storage. You initialize your Terraform project using terraform init. Since you haven't specified any backend configuration, Terraform will use the local backend by default. You then add some configurations for your CloudOptic resources in your .tf files. Running terraform apply will execute these configurations, and the resulting state will be stored in a terraform.tfstate file in your project directory.

Transitioning to Other Backends

While the local backend is excellent for initial exploration or smaller setups, its limitations become apparent as you scale. Fortunately, transitioning from a local backend to a different type of backend like AWS S3 is straightforward. You specify the new backend in your Terraform configuration and then reinitialize your project. Terraform will prompt you to copy the existing state to the new backend.

Overall, the local backend serves as a foundational building block in your Terraform journey. It offers a straightforward way to manage state files but should be used judiciously, considering its limitations in terms of scalability and security.

State Locking and Unlocking

An integral part of state locking is its ability to avoid data conflicts that can arise from running multiple processes in parallel. This is of the utmost importance in collaborative settings because numerous individuals may be executing Terraform commands at the same time. At all times, the locking mechanism makes sure that no two operations that can change the state are running in parallel. If state locking wasn't in place, running multiple operations at once could corrupt data or lead to errors caused by inconsistent state files.

How State Locking Works?

The principle of state locking is simple. Terraform gets a lock on the state file whenever a state-modifying action begins. Once the lock is freed, all further operations that could modify the state file can proceed. Consider the following scenario: one user is executing terraform apply; until that operation finishes and the lock is released, another user cannot execute terraform apply or terraform destruct.

Locking in Local Backend

Terraform manages state locking by creating a lock file in the context of the local backend. In the same directory as the state file, a lock file is created when an operation starts. This file is usually titled terraform.tfstate.lock. The operation is released from the lock when this file is removed.

Sample Program: Getting Local Backend Locked

Below is how to simulate state locking while dealing with a CloudOptic configuration:

- Launch two separate terminal windows. In each, go to the directory where your Terraform project is located.
- Terraform Plan should be executed in the first terminal. The modifications should not be confirmed.

- Try executing terraform apply on the second terminal while terraform plan is active in the first. There is a feature in Terraform that lets you know when the lock is released.

To show how locking works, following is a simple script:

```
#!/bin/bash


# Acquire lock manually

echo "Locking state file..."

touch terraform.tfstate.lock


# Simulate long-running operation

echo "Simulating a long-running operation..."

sleep 30


# Release lock

echo "Releasing lock..."

rm terraform.tfstate.lock
```

Run this script in one terminal, and while it's executing, try running terraform apply in another terminal. You'll notice the apply operation will wait until the lock file is removed.

Unlocking State File

In some scenarios, a lock may not be released automatically. For instance, if a Terraform operation is interrupted or crashes, the lock file may remain in place. In such cases, manual intervention is required to delete the lock file.

Following is a simple manual unlock Script:

```
#!/bin/bash

# Safety check before removing the lock file

if [ -f "terraform.tfstate.lock" ]; then

 echo "Manually unlocking the state file..."

 rm terraform.tfstate.lock

else

 echo "No lock file found."

fi
```

By running this script, you remove the state lock, enabling other operations to proceed.

To sum up, state locking is crucial for team settings and other situations when Terraform processes must go smoothly without conflicts. The local backend does have some simple locking features, but when you start to scale and need more advanced methods, you will probably switch to using remote backends.

Backend and Cloud Integration

When you use Terraform's backend integration, your local environment can talk to a storage system in the cloud. With this integration, you can safely save the state file and use the cloud storage solutions' state locking and encryption features for team collaboration. Within this framework, we will get into the process of integrating a backend such as AWS S3 with your CloudOptic setup.

Relationship between Backend and Cloud

The Terraform backend, which can be set up to reside on a cloud service, is in charge of managing states. Azure Blob Storage, Amazon Simple Storage Service, and Google Cloud Storage are a few examples of popular backends. In addition to hosting the state file, the cloud-based backend frequently offers features like versioning, state locking, and encryption at rest.

Sample Program: Integrate AWS S3 Backend

Since you already have an AWS account, AWS CLI installed and configured on your machine, following are the steps for the integration process:

- First, create an S3 bucket where the Terraform state file will be stored.

```
aws s3api create-bucket --bucket my-cloudoptic-terraform-state --region us-west-2
```

- You may enable versioning as it is optional but highly recommended for state file versioning.

```
aws s3api put-bucket-versioning --bucket my-cloudoptic-terraform-state --versioning-configuration Status=Enabled
```

- Modify your Terraform configuration (main.tf) to use the S3 backend.

```
terraform {
 backend "s3" {
 bucket = "my-cloudoptic-terraform-state"
 key = "state"
 region = "us-west-2"
 }
}
```

- Run terraform init to initialize the new backend configuration. If you have an existing local state file (terraform.tfstate), Terraform will prompt you to transfer it to the new S3 backend.
- Accept the migration to migrate the state.
- Verify that everything is working as expected by running terraform plan and terraform apply.

```
terraform plan
terraform apply
```

To sum up, it is possible to take advantage of the cloud's extensive feature set for managing the state file by linking your backend with cloud storage solutions such as AWS S3. Collaboratively managing infrastructure with this architecture ensures a high degree of reliability and security.

Remote State Backend and Options

There are a number of different kinds of state backends in the Terraform ecosystem, but they all do the same thing: they store and maintain Terraform's state files. State files can be stored on your local system by local backends or on remote services by remote state backends. Improved version control, security, and team communication are all benefits of using remote backends.

Here we'll take a look at Terraform Cloud and Consul, two rather popular remote state backend choices.

Terraform Cloud as a Remote Backend

Terraform Cloud is a SaaS (Software as a Service) product offered by HashiCorp, the same company behind Terraform. It provides various features to enhance the capabilities of Terraform, such as state storage, remote runs, and a private registry for sharing modules. It serves as a centralized workspace for deploying and managing your infrastructure.

Key Features

- State Storage: Stores the Terraform state file in an encrypted format, ensuring that sensitive data is secure.
- Team Collaboration: Allows multiple team members to run terraform plan and terraform apply, which enhances productivity.
- Versioning and Audit Trail: Provides an inbuilt version control mechanism for the state file, as well as detailed logs for tracking changes.

Sample Configuration

To use Terraform Cloud as a backend, specify it in your main.tf:

```
terraform {

 backend "remote" {

 hostname = "app.terraform.io"

 organization = "my-org"
```

```
workspaces {
name = "my-workspace"
}
}
}
```

Run terraform init to initialize the backend, and proceed with terraform plan and terraform apply as usual.

Consul as a Remote Backend

Consul is another product from HashiCorp designed for service discovery and key-value storage. It can also be used as a remote state backend for Terraform. Unlike Terraform Cloud, Consul is generally self-hosted, which gives you control over your environment.

Key Features

- State Locking: Consul allows for distributed locking, ensuring that only one instance of Terraform can modify the state at any given time.
- Data Center Aware: Being a tool designed for high availability, Consul can replicate state files across multiple data centers.
- Security: You can utilize ACLs (Access Control Lists) to provide secure access to the state files.

Sample Configuration

To configure Consul as your backend, update your main.tf as follows:

```
terraform {
backend "consul" {
address = "consul.example.com"
path = "terraform-state/prod"
}
```

```
}
```

Run terraform init to initialize the new backend. The state will now be stored in Consul at the specified path.

Terraform Cloud vs. Consul

- Terraform Cloud provides a user-friendly interface, making it more straightforward for those who are new to Terraform. Consul, on the other hand, requires a deeper understanding of its architecture.
- Terraform Cloud offers both free and paid tiers, while Consul can incur operational costs if you're self-hosting.
- Consul is more suited for large-scale, complex systems with multiple data centers, but this comes at the expense of ease of use and setup.
- Consul offers more control and customization options, given it's self-hosted. Terraform Cloud is more opinionated, focusing on convenience and rapid deployment.

Both these options offer benefits that could be leveraged depending on your specific needs. Terraform Cloud's user-friendly interface and remote runs might be beneficial for teams that are new to IaC, while Consul's high availability and data center awareness are excellent for more complex setups.

Backend Configuration

A wide variety of AWS services, such as Elastic Compute Cloud (EC2) instances, Relational Database Service (RDS) databases, and Simple Storage Service (S3) buckets, are necessary to run CloudOptic. Using a remote backend to store the Terraform state is not only easy for such a complete configuration, but it is often critical for team collaboration, versioning, and security.

Assume for a moment that CloudOptic has decided to use AWS S3 and Terraform Cloud as their remote backends. A key role can be played by HashiCorp's tools in both instances.

Given below are the detailed instructions for setting each one up.

Using Terraform Cloud with CloudOptic

- Sign up for a Terraform Cloud account.
- Within Terraform Cloud, create a workspace named cloudoptic.
- Navigate to "User Settings" to generate an API token for authentication.

- In your Terraform code for CloudOptic, update the main.tf or create a backend.tf file with the following configuration:

```
terraform {

 backend "remote" {

 hostname = "app.terraform.io"

 organization = "your-org-name"


 workspaces {

 name = "cloudoptic"

 }

 }

}
```

- Set the TFE_TOKEN environment variable in your shell or CI/CD pipeline using the API token generated earlier.
- Run terraform init.

Using AWS S3 with CloudOptic:

- Log into your AWS Management Console and create a new S3 bucket named cloudoptic-terraform-state.
- Under the "Properties" tab for your S3 bucket, enable versioning to keep a history of your state files.
- For state locking and consistency, create a DynamoDB table named cloudoptic-terraform-locks.
- Similar to Terraform Cloud, add or update the backend configuration in your main.tf or backend.tf as follows:

```
terraform {

 backend "s3" {

 bucket = "cloudoptic-terraform-state"

 key = "terraform.tfstate"

 region = "us-west-2"

 dynamodb_table = "cloudoptic-terraform-locks"

 }

}
```

- Ensure your AWS credentials are set either in the environment variables AWS_ACCESS_KEY_ID and AWS_SECRET_ACCESS_KEY or via any other AWS credential method.
- Run terraform init.

Both of these backend configurations are designed to work seamlessly with HashiCorp's other tools. For instance, if CloudOptic is using Consul for service discovery or Vault for secret management, the Terraform Cloud workspace can integrate with these tools for a more unified infrastructure management experience. Similarly, AWS services like AWS Key Management Service (KMS) can be used for additional layers of security for the S3 backend.

Whom to Choose?

If your organization is deeply invested in AWS services, utilizing S3 as a backend could offer tighter integration with other AWS resources. If you're looking for an all-in-one solution for not just state management but also CI/CD pipelines and collaboration, Terraform Cloud could be a better fit.

Considerations like infrastructure size, development team composition, and individual regulatory mandates may influence the final choice. Both options are top-notch, and the final pick ought to be in harmony with the overarching objectives of the company and its architecture.

Managing Resource Drift

Many enterprises have resource drift while controlling IaC, particularly with powerful cloud setups such as CloudOptic. The term "drift" is used to describe the gradual separation between the actual and configured states of your resources in your Terraform files. As an example, drift may occur if the Terraform state file was not updated whenever an engineer added an EC2 instance manually through the AWS console.

In order to provide its services, CloudOptic probably depends on a specific setup of resources. Particularly detrimental in this context is drift, which may create needless expenditures, diminished performance, or even security holes. S3 buckets, EC2 instances, and RDS databases are all AWS resources that even a minor configuration error can have a major effect on CloudOptic.

Tools and Techniques for Detecting Drift

Terraform Refresh

The most straightforward way to detect drift is to run terraform refresh. The local state file is updated with real-world infrastructure information by running this command. But it won't alter the system files or the infrastructure in any way. Just run this command in the directory of your CloudOptic Terraform workspace to make it CloudOptic specific.

Terraform Plan

If you want to find drift, you can run a terraform plan to see how the current state compares to the configuration files. To assist you find inconsistencies, it gives a thorough list of what Terraform will do.

Sample Program: Detect and Manage Drift

Let us say the AWS EC2 instance is managed by Terraform for the CloudOptic application. You can detect and manage drift through the following steps:

Detecting Drift

- Imagine that someone manually stops the EC2 instance via the AWS Console.
- Navigate to the directory where your CloudOptic' Terraform files are stored. Run terraform refresh to update the local state file.
- Execute terraform plan. If there is drift, you'll see output indicating the difference between the configuration and the real-world state.

Managing Drift

- One way to fix the drift is to manually restart the EC2 instance and then run terraform refresh again to sync the state file.
- Alternatively, you can modify the Terraform configuration to match the new state and run terraform apply.

- To prevent future drift, you might establish stricter access controls on your AWS resources or implement an alerting mechanism that notifies you of manual changes.

Following is a simple bash script that you can schedule to run periodically to check for drift specifically for your CloudOptic setup.

```
#!/bin/bash

# Navigate to CloudOptic Terraform workspace
cd /path/to/cloudoptic/terraform/workspace

# Update local state file
terraform refresh

# Run plan and output to a file
terraform plan -out=plan.out

# Check if there is any drift
if grep -q "0 to add, 0 to change, 0 to destroy" plan.out; then
 echo "No drift detected."
else
 echo "Drift detected. Please review the Terraform plan."
 # Insert your alerting mechanism here, e.g., send an email or Slack message
fi
```

```
# Clean up

rm plan.out
```

In the next section, you might also consider integrating such drift detection scripts into a CI/CD pipeline, perhaps running the script automatically upon each merge to the main branch of your Terraform code repository.

Integrate Drift Detection into CI/CD

A perfect automation solution for a cloud service like CloudOptic would be to incorporate drift detection scripts into a Continuous Integration/Continuous Deployment (CI/CD) pipeline. It does a real-time check to ensure your infrastructure is in sync with your Terraform configuration files. I'll show you step-by-step how to do this.

The first step is to have all your Terraform scripts in a version control system like Git. This allows your CI/CD pipeline to fetch the most recent versions of your code. If you're using Jenkins, create a new pipeline. In GitLab CI/CD, this would involve adding a .gitlab-ci.yml file to your repository. In GitHub, you could set this up under GitHub Actions.

Terraform Initialization

You want to start by initializing Terraform as the first step in your pipeline. This will download all required providers and modules for your CloudOptic setup.

```
# Example using GitLab CI/CD

stages:

 - init

 - plan

 - apply


init:
```

```
script:

 - terraform init
```

Drift Detection Script

Now, we will move on to integrating the drift detection script we previously learned. The script will first perform a terraform refresh to sync the local state with the real-world infrastructure. It will then run terraform plan to detect any drift.

```
# Drift Detection script, save as drift_detection.sh

#!/bin/bash


# Navigate to the workspace directory

cd /path/to/terraform


# Refresh Terraform state

terraform refresh


# Run Terraform plan and capture output

terraform plan > plan_output.txt


# Check for drift

if grep -q "No changes. Infrastructure is up-to-date." plan_output.txt; then

 echo "No drift detected."

else
```

```
 echo "Drift detected."
 exit 1
fi
```

Add this script to your CI/CD pipeline configuration:

```
# Add to existing GitLab CI/CD configuration
detect_drift:
 stage: plan
 script:
 - chmod +x drift_detection.sh
 - ./drift_detection.sh
```

Conditional Apply

You can make the terraform apply conditional, based on the result of the drift detection script.

```
apply_changes:
 stage: apply
 script:
 - terraform apply -auto-approve
 only:
 variables:
 - $DRIFT_DETECTED == "false"
```

Notification

You might want to alert the responsible team when drift is detected. This could be an email, a Slack message, or even an automated ticket creation.

```
# Adding alerting to the drift_detection.sh

...

# Check for drift

if grep -q "No changes. Infrastructure is up-to-date." plan_output.txt; then

 echo "No drift detected."

else

 echo "Drift detected."

 # Add code here to send Slack message or email

 exit 1

fi
```

After you've followed all these steps, the procedure will be fully automated and integrated. Making sure there is no slop in your configuration is crucial because CloudOptic has to keep a tight infrastructure for best service quality. You may concentrate on improving features or expanding your services while the CI/CD pipeline monitors your infrastructure in real-time.

Secrets Management

Securely storing, distributing, and managing sensitive data such as API keys, passwords, and certificates is the main focus of secrets management, a subfield of information security. Because secrets are so crucial to your cloud architecture, it is imperative that you comprehend their handling in the context of Terraform and CloudOptic.

Why It Matters?

Protected data is frequently required by Terraform scripts in order to provision resources. Nevertheless, there are a number of dangers, such as the possibility of data leaks and illegal access, that you run when you save this information in plain text within your scripts or state files. It is very critical to guarantee the secure management of these "secrets," particularly in automated settings like as CI/CD pipelines.

Basic Secrets Handling Methods

One of the straightforward ways to handle secrets is by setting them as environment variables. Terraform will automatically read any environment variables that start with TF_VAR_, which you can then use within your configuration.

```
export TF_VAR_secret_key="mysecretkey"
```

And in your Terraform script:

```
variable "secret_key" {}
```

You can prompt for secret data at runtime using input variables. This method bypasses storing secrets in the state file but could be cumbersome for automation.

```
variable "secret_key" {

 description = "Enter your secret key"

 sensitive = true

}
```

Terraform will prompt you to input the value when you run terraform apply.

Advanced Secrets Management

For a more robust and production-grade option, consider using a Key Management System (KMS) like AWS KMS, Azure Key Vault, or HashiCorp's Vault. These systems will store the secrets in an encrypted format and allow you to access them dynamically.

With AWS KMS, you can use a Customer Master Key (CMK) to encrypt the secrets.

```
data "aws_kms_secrets" "example" {

 secret {

 name = "secret_key"

 payload = "EncryptedPayload"
```

```
}
}
```

Vault is another powerful tool for secrets management, where secrets can be read dynamically into your Terraform script.

```
data "vault_generic_secret" "example" {
 path = "secret/my_secrets"
}


resource "cloudoptic_instance" "example" {
 secret_key = data.vault_generic_secret.example.data["secret_key"]
}
```

Sensitive State Files

Even if you're not storing secrets in plain text, Terraform's state files could still contain sensitive data. This is another aspect to consider. While Terraform has the sensitive argument to mark a variable as sensitive, it's crucial to know that it doesn't prevent the sensitive data from being stored in the state file.

To avoid this:

- You can store your state files in an encrypted S3 bucket if you're using AWS or other equivalent options in different cloud providers.
- Backends like Azure Blob Storage or AWS S3 can be configured to store the state files in an encrypted form.
- Platforms like AWS offer object-level encryption, further providing an additional layer of security to your state files.

Through a well-thought-out secrets management strategy, you ensure a highly secure, automated, and efficient operation for your CloudOptic deployments, substantially reducing the risk of unintended data exposure.

Encrypt State Files

You must encrypt Terraform state files if you want to protect your infrastructure when dealing with cloud services that could store sensitive data. Encrypting state files prevents unauthorized parties from accessing the information while it is in transit or at rest.

Setting Up Encrypted Storage

To store your Terraform state files in an encrypted S3 bucket, follow these steps:

Create an Encrypted S3 Bucket

In the AWS Management Console, go to the S3 service and create a new bucket. Under the "Server-side encryption" option, choose "Enable." Select the encryption method, either AWS-managed keys (SSE-S3) or KMS.

Terraform Backend Configuration

In your main Terraform configuration file, you can specify the S3 bucket as your backend for storing state files. Add the following backend configuration:

```
terraform {

 backend "s3" {

 bucket = "my-encrypted-bucket"

 key = "path/to/state/file"

 region = "us-west-2"

 encrypt = true

 }

}
```

In this configuration, encrypt = true ensures that the stored state files will be encrypted.

Utilizing AWS KMS

You can create a custom Customer Master Key (CMK) and specify it in your S3 bucket encryption options.

- In the AWS Management Console, navigate to KMS and create a new key. Define the administrative and usage permissions for the key.
- Go back to your S3 bucket and modify its encryption settings to use the KMS key you've just created.
- Add kms_key_id attribute to the backend configuration.

```
terraform {
 backend "s3" {
 // ... existing settings
 kms_key_id = "arn:aws:kms:region:account-id:key/key-id"
 }
}
```

Configuring Resource with Encrypted State Files

You want to configure a CloudOptic resource and you want to ensure that the Terraform state for this is securely stored. Your Terraform code for setting up a CloudOptic resource might look something like this:

```
provider "cloudoptic" {
 api_key = var.api_key
}

resource "cloudoptic_my_resource" "example" {
 // resource configurations
}
```

Use environment variables or a secrets management service like AWS Secrets Manager to manage the CloudOptic api_key. Do not hardcode it in your Terraform files. After setting up your backend and CloudOptic provider, initialize your Terraform directory:

```
terraform init
```

This will set up the S3 backend and store the state files in encrypted form. Now you can safely run terraform apply or other commands, knowing that your state files will be encrypted and stored securely in AWS S3.

Backing Up State Files

Depending on where your state files are stored—either on a local backend or a remote backend like Terraform Cloud or Consul—backup methods will differ.

Following are the different strategies:

Local Backend Backups

Manual Copy

For local backends, the simplest backup strategy is to manually copy the .tfstate files to a secure backup location. This approach may suffice for smaller setups but isn't scalable.

Version Control Systems

You can also use a Version Control System like Git to track changes in your .tfstate file. While not recommended for storing sensitive data, you can still encrypt the file before pushing it into a repository.

Scripted Backups

Automated backup scripts can also be helpful. A Bash or Python script can be scheduled to run at regular intervals to copy the .tfstate files to a secure backup location.

Terraform Cloud Backups

Terraform Cloud offers automatic backup of your state files. However, for an added layer of security:

You can use Terraform Cloud's API to download the current state file. Below is a simple curl command to do this:

```
curl \
```

```
--header "Authorization: Bearer $TOKEN" \
--header "Content-Type: application/vnd.api+json" \
"https://app.terraform.io/api/v2/workspaces/$WORKSPACE_ID/current-state-version" > backup.tfstate
```

Replace $TOKEN and $WORKSPACE_ID with your actual Terraform Cloud token and workspace ID, respectively.

Consul Backend Backups

Snapshot Mechanism

Consul provides a snapshot mechanism to back up the entire key-value store, which would include your Terraform state files if stored there. Run:

```
consul snapshot save backup.snap
```

Manual Copy from KV Store

You can also manually copy the state files from the Consul KV store to a secure location. This can be scripted using Consul's API or CLI.

If you follow these steps, you can save your Terraform state files locally, in Terraform Cloud, or in Consul, and you'll always have a backup that can be restored if something happens to the original. This will guarantee that your CloudOptic deployments are managed resiliently.

Summary

The chapter covered the many ways to back up Terraform state files, based on whether they are stored in the local backend, Terraform Cloud, or Consul. Manually copying.tfstate files, using a version control system like Git, or setting up automated backup scripts were the three approaches described for local backends. Contrarily, Terraform Cloud provides automated backups of state files; however, you may take it a step further by retrieving the most recent state files through Terraform Cloud's API.

The snapshot approach is useful for users of the Consul backend since it encapsulates the Terraform state files and allows backup of the full key-value store. Alternatives include using a third-party tool, such as consul-backinator, or manually copying from the KV store. It was suggested that CloudOptic use a mix of API-based and scheduled backups to reliably save the most current state files when implementing these methods.

You were provided with detailed instructions, code samples, and recommendations for best practices throughout the chapter to help you develop your backup plan. You may better manage your CloudOptic resources with resilience if you are familiar with these various backup solutions and can use them to avoid unintentional data loss. From simple installations to massive rollouts, we kept a holistic approach to accommodate all kinds of requirements and complexity. With this information in hand, you can build a solid disaster recovery plan for any business, no matter how big or little.

Test Exercise

1. What are the three methods learned for backing up state files in a local backend?
    a. Automated backup scripts, manual copy, API-based
    b. Manual copy, version control, automated backup scripts
    c. API-based, Terraform Cloud, Consul snapshots
    d. Version control, Consul snapshots, Terraform Cloud
2. Which API is used to pull current state files from Terraform Cloud?
    a. GET /statefile
    b. POST /statefile
    c. GET /state/version
    d. PUT /statefile
3. What does the consul-backinator tool do?
    a. Encrypts Consul keys
    b. Backs up the Consul key-value store
    c. Deploys Consul clusters
    d. Monitors Consul nodes
4. Which of these is NOT a method for backing up Terraform state files in Consul?
    a. Consul snapshots
    b. Manual copying from the KV store
    c. Using terraform state pull
    d. Using consul-backinator
5. In the context of CloudOptic, what combination of backup methods was suggested for the most reliable backup?

a. API-based and scheduled backups
b. Manual copying and version control
c. Consul snapshots and version control
d. Scheduled backups and manual copying

6. What command would you use to create a backup of your .tfstate file locally?
    a. terraform backup
    b. terraform state backup
    c. Manual copy of .tfstate file
    d. terraform state mv
7. What can be a potential risk if you don't back up your .tfstate files?
    a. Exceeding API rate limits
    b. Accidental data loss
    c. Increased financial costs
    d. Deprecation of resources
8. Which backend offers automatic state file backups?
    a. Local backend
    b. Consul
    c. Terraform Cloud
    d. All of the above
9. What is the purpose of encrypting your .tfstate files?
    a. To prevent unauthorized access
    b. To reduce the file size
    c. To improve performance
    d. To make it easier to version control
10. What could be a benefit of integrating backup scripts into your CI/CD pipeline?
    a. Reduced need for monitoring
    b. Automated backup process
    c. Lower financial costs
    d. Reduced API rate limits

CHAPTER 5: ADVANCED CONFIGURATION TECHNIQUES

Advanced Terraform Overview

We will dive into some of the more complex but essential parts of Terraform in Chapter 5, with the goal of becoming experts in using this infrastructure as a tool for writing code. The components we will examine cover a wide array of features provided by Terraform:

- Protected Secret Injection: When working with IaC, it's essential to handle sensitive data safely, such as API keys and passwords. With secure secret injection, you may confidently incorporate this kind of data into your Terraform configurations.
- Collections: Lists, maps, and sets are examples of collections that can be worked with in Terraform. Data management and complicated infrastructures rely on a thorough understanding of collections.
- Resource Addressing: It is critical to be able to recognize and work with individual Terraform resources. With resource addressing, you can zero in on specific resources or sets of resources to apply, destroy, or manipulate state-wise.
- Terraform Functions: These are in-built functions that make it easier to format data, manipulate data, and do other logical tasks. When it comes to tweaking and improving Terraform setups, they are crucial.
- Configuration-Based Conditional Logic: Your infrastructure setup is likely to be complex most of the time. You can add decision-making capabilities to your setups in Terraform using conditional logic.

Our CloudOptic case study will serve as a practical example as we delve into these issues. We will tackle these qualities from both a theoretical and a practical perspective, with an eye towards their practical use. The goal is to ensure you know how to use these principles in your own work with CloudOptic and Terraform.

Secure Secret Injection

The term "secret injection" describes the practice of safely inserting private information into your Terraform settings, such as API keys, credentials, and other sensitive data. This is of the utmost importance because it is both insecure and against best practices to hardcode such information directly into your configuration files. To inject these secrets in a more organized and secure way, you can use HashiCorp's products like Vault.

Significance of Secret Injection

Your house keys are like a secret; you wouldn't just leave them laying around. Similarly, you should not store sensitive data in your Terraform codebase. Some examples of such things are API keys for cloud providers, certificates, and database credentials. Any number of dangers, such as data breaches and illegal access, might result from hardcoding such information and making it accessible to unauthorized individuals.

Function of the HashiCorp Vault

For secure data storage, HashiCorp's Vault is a top pick. It has a secure location to keep secrets and an extensive API for creating new secrets on the fly. The possibilities of Vault are vast and varied, including secret rolling, secret revocation, secret leasing, and the power to break glass in an emergency. Vault can be easily integrated with your current infrastructure code because it is Terraform compliant.

Setting up Vault

Assuming you have Vault installed, start a dev server using the following command:

```
vault server -dev
```

This will give you a temporary Vault environment. Take note of the root token displayed; you'll need it to interact with Vault.

Run the following commands to authenticate and write secrets:

```
vault login [Your-Root-Token-Here]

vault kv put secret/cloudoptic api_key="YOUR-API-KEY"
```

Injecting Secrets

To utilize these secrets in Terraform, you'll have to specify Vault as a provider in your configuration. This is similar to how you specify other providers like AWS or GCP.

```
provider "vault" {

 address = "http://127.0.0.1:8200"

 token = "Your-Root-Token-Here"

}
```

Retrieving Secrets

You can then use the Vault provider to fetch these secrets and use them in your resources.

```
data "vault_generic_secret" "cloudoptic_api_key" {
 path = "secret/cloudoptic"
}

resource "example_resource" "example" {
 api_key = data.vault_generic_secret.cloudoptic_api_key.data["api_key"]
}
```

Using Secrets

Assume you have a CloudOptic resource that requires an API key. You can inject this key from Vault.

```
resource "cloudoptic_security_policy" "example" {
 name = "example-policy"
 api_key = data.vault_generic_secret.cloudoptic_api_key.data["api_key"]
}
```

Vault also provides the ability to generate dynamic secrets, secrets that are generated on-the-fly and have a lease period. This ensures that no static secret lives for long, reducing the chance of unauthorized access. To use dynamic secrets, you'd set up Vault roles and policies and then update your Terraform configurations to request these dynamic secrets.

While this overview provides the basic building blocks to get you started, Vault offers many more features like ACL policies, secret versioning, and audit logs, which you can explore to fit your specific requirements.

Collection and Structural Types

Collections are a special kind of data structure in Terraform that may store more than one value. Their importance becomes paramount when handling infrastructure components that are either repetitive or subject to change. Common representations of structural types include object and tuple types, while lists, sets, and maps are used to classify collections.

Lists

Lists are ordered collections of items of the same type. For example, a list can hold multiple strings or multiple integers but not a mix.

A number of security policies are available in CloudOptic that you would like to establish. A list containing these policy names could be declared.

```
locals {

 policies = ["policy_1", "policy_2", "policy_3"]

}
```

Sets

Sets are like lists, but they are unordered and cannot have duplicate values. Sets are ideal when you want to ensure every item is unique and the order does not matter.

Suppose you have different modules for network segmentation in CloudOptic, and each one has a unique ID. You can use a set to ensure there are no duplicates.

```
locals {

 module_ids = toset(["id_1", "id_2", "id_3"])

}
```

Maps

Maps are collections that associate a key with a value. The keys must be unique, and each key's value is accessible by referencing its key.

You could use a map to associate CloudOptic policy names with their corresponding IDs.

```
locals {
```

```
policy_map = {

"policy_1" = "id_1",

"policy_2" = "id_2"

}

}
```

Objects

Objects allow you to combine multiple types into a single, complex type. Each attribute of an object can be of any type.

For example, you need to provide the name, priority, and action of a CloudOptic security rule among its many attributes.

```
locals {

security_rule = {

name = "rule_1"

priority = 1

action = "allow"

}

}
```

Tuples

Tuples are collections of arbitrary but known element types. Unlike lists and sets, tuples can contain elements of different types but have a fixed length.

Assume there is a tuple that contains a CloudOptic rule name, rule ID, and a Boolean to indicate if it's enabled or not.

```
locals {
```

```
rule_tuple = ["rule_1", "id_1", true]
}
```

Sample Program: Using Collections and Structural Types

Given below is a comprehensive example that incorporates collections and structural types to manage CloudOptic policies and rules.

```
locals {
policies = ["policy_1", "policy_2"]
policy_map = {
"policy_1" = "id_1",
"policy_2" = "id_2"
}
security_rules = [
{
name = "rule_1"
priority = 1
action = "allow"
},
{
name = "rule_2"
priority = 2
action = "deny"
```

```
}
]
}

resource "cloudoptic_policy" "example" {
 count = length(local.policies)
 name = local.policies[count.index]
}

resource "cloudoptic_rule" "example" {
 for_each = { for rule in local.security_rules : rule.name => rule }

 name = each.value.name
 priority = each.value.priority
 action = each.value.action
}
```

In the above sample program, we used a list to define the names of CloudOptic policies and a map to associate policy names with their IDs. We used an object type within a list to specify multiple security rules with various attributes. These types help you compartmentalize data, ensuring that your configurations are not only more human-readable but also easier to maintain and scale.

Resource Addressing and Usage

Resource addressing is a powerful feature in Terraform that allows you to explicitly refer to a resource within a Terraform configuration. This is particularly useful for actions like resource targeting, dependencies, and output references.

Syntax

The common syntax for a resource address is:

```
[provider][resource_type].[resource_name]
```

For instance, if you have an AWS EC2 instance named web_server, the resource address would be aws_instance.web_server. This is the absolute address, but there are also relative addresses, such as self, which refers to the resource where the address is being used.

Qualified Resource Address

A more complex form of resource addressing includes specifying a module or a resource count index, making the reference more specific. Given below is the syntax:

```
module.[module_name].[provider][resource_type].[resource_name]
```

or with an index:

```
[provider][resource_type].[resource_name][index]
```

Sample Program: Establishing Dependency

Assume you are required to establish a Security Group and a Virtual Private Cloud (VPC) on behalf of CloudOptic, which is providing cloud services through Amazon Web Services (AWS). You would utilize resource addressing to establish the dependency between the Security Group and the VPC.

The following is an example of how to set up a VPC and Security Group in Terraform:

```
resource "aws_vpc" "cloudoptic_vpc" {

 cidr_block = "10.0.0.0/16"

}
```

```
resource "aws_security_group" "cloudoptic_sg" {

 name = "cloudoptic-sg"

 description = "CloudOptic Security Group"

 vpc_id = aws_vpc.cloudoptic_vpc.id

}
```

In the above sample program, the Security Group resource (aws_security_group.cloudoptic_sg) has a vpc_id attribute that uses the resource address of the VPC (aws_vpc.cloudoptic_vpc.id) to create a dependency. This ensures that Terraform creates the VPC before the Security Group.

For Targeted Actions

Another important aspect is the ability to perform actions on a specific resource. For instance, if you need to apply changes only to the Security Group, you could use:

```
terraform apply -target=aws_security_group.cloudoptic_sg
```

This action will only affect the Security Group resource, leaving all other resources untouched. It is particularly useful for isolating changes and reducing the scope of operations.

For Outputs

You might want to output the VPC's ID and Security Group's ID in the CloudOptic dashboard. Resource addressing helps here as well:

```
output "vpc_id" {

 value = aws_vpc.cloudoptic_vpc.id

}



output "security_group_id" {

 value = aws_security_group.cloudoptic_sg.id
```

```
}
```

The resource addresses are used to fetch specific values for these output variables, and this information could be crucial for debugging or for connecting services in CloudOptic.

For Data Sources

The addressing of resources is also helpful for data sources. So, we will pretend an EC2 instance requires CloudOptic to retrieve an Amazon Machine Image (AMI).

```
data "aws_ami" "example" {

 most_recent = true

 owners = ["amazon"]

 ...

}



resource "aws_instance" "cloudoptic_instance" {

 ami = data.aws_ami.example.id

 ...

}
```

In the above sample program, data.aws_ami.example.id is used as a resource address to fetch the most recent AMI ID for the EC2 instance.

To sum up, resource addressing allows for greater precision when specifying operations, dependencies, and values within Terraform configurations. This becomes an integral part of infrastructure management, particularly in complex setups like those you would encounter with CloudOptic.

Functions in Terraform

An integral part of every Terraform configuration file is the functions that allow you to work with data and parameters. Data processing, filtering, and calculating are only a few examples of when they're useful. The most common way to employ functions in expressions is to pass in an argument or arguments and have them return a predefined value.

Categories of Functions

Terraform functions fall under several categories:

- Numeric Functions: Used for mathematical operations. Examples are abs, ceil, floor.
- String Functions: Manipulate text strings. Examples include substr, join, format.
- Collection Functions: Work on lists, sets, or maps. Functions like length, element, lookup are common here.
- Logical Functions: Deal with Boolean logic. Functions such as and, or, not fit into this category.
- Encoding Functions: Useful for data encoding. base64encode, jsonencode are examples.
- Time Functions: Handle time-based values, like timeadd, timestamp.

The syntax of using a function in Terraform is pretty straightforward:

```
function_name(arg1, arg2, ...)
```

We'll explore these functions in more detail by looking at how they apply to the CloudOptic situation.

Numeric Functions

Suppose CloudOptic needs to automatically scale its AWS EC2 instances based on CPU utilization. We can use the ceil function to ensure that the number of instances is a whole number:

```
resource "aws_autoscaling_group" "cloudoptic_asg" {

 desired_capacity = ceil(var.average_cpu_utilization / 10)

 ...

}
```

In this case, ceil rounds up the number to ensure that sufficient instances are available for handling the load.

String Functions

String functions can be particularly useful for formatting tags or resource names:

```
resource "aws_instance" "cloudoptic_instance" {

 tags = {

 Name = format("CloudOptic-%s", var.environment)

 }

 ...

}
```

The format function takes the environment variable and appends it to the string "CloudOptic-" to create the resource name dynamically.

Collection Functions

Collection functions like element can be instrumental in managing collections, such as lists of security groups:

```
resource "aws_instance" "cloudoptic_instance" {

 security_groups = [

 element(var.security_groups, 0),

 element(var.security_groups, 1)

 ]

 ...

}
```

Here, element fetches specific security groups from the list based on their index.

Logical Functions

Logical functions are useful when you need to conditionally create resources:

```
resource "aws_instance" "cloudoptic_instance" {

 count = var.create_instance ? 1 : 0

 ...

}
```

Here, the aws_instance will only be created if var.create_instance is true.

Encoding Functions

If CloudOptic requires to encode some data in Base64 format for secure transmission, you can use base64encode:

```
resource "aws_instance" "cloudoptic_instance" {

 user_data – base64encode(var.user_data_script)

 ...

}
```

Time Functions

Suppose CloudOptic needs to schedule an EC2 instance for backup:

```
locals {

 backup_time = timeadd(timestamp(), "2h")

}
```

Here, timeadd adds 2 hours to the current time, which can be used to schedule backups.

Function Nesting

Terraform also allows for nesting functions to create more complex expressions:

```
locals {

 complete_tag = format("CloudOptic-%s-%s", upper(var.environment), timestamp())

}
```

Both upper and timestamp functions are nested within the format function to create a complete tag that includes the upper-case environment name and a timestamp.

You may handle and control data in your Terraform settings effectively by exploiting these varied kinds of functions. A scalable and adaptive environment, such as CloudOptic, requires dynamic, flexible, and intelligent IaC, which may be achieved through the exploitation of these functions.

Built-in Dependency Management

Like all IaC tools, Terraform relies on dependency management. To guarantee the correct sequence of resource creation, modification, or destruction, it painstakingly resolves dependencies. Both explicit and implicit dependencies are part of Terraform's dependency management.

Explicit Dependencies

Explicit dependencies in Terraform are declared using the depends_on argument. By explicitly defining dependencies, you tell Terraform to wait for a certain resource to be created before it proceeds to the next one.

Now, we will make up that CloudOptic has a VPC and that an EC2 instance ought to be a part of this VPC. The VPC is crucial in this case for the EC2 instance.

```
resource "aws_vpc" "cloudoptic_vpc" {

 cidr_block = "10.0.0.0/16"

}



resource "aws_instance" "cloudoptic_instance" {

 ami = "ami-abc12345"
```

```
instance_type = "t2.micro"


depends_on = [
aws_vpc.cloudoptic_vpc
]
}
```

In the above code snippet, the depends_on argument ensures that the VPC must be created before the EC2 instance.

Implicit Dependencies

Implicit dependencies occur automatically based on resource configurations. Terraform's graph-based architecture can understand which resources are dependent on which, even without explicit declarations.

Let us say CloudOptic needs to associate a security group with an EC2 instance. The security group itself relies on a VPC.

```
resource "aws_security_group" "cloudoptic_sg" {
name = "cloudoptic-sg"
vpc_id = aws_vpc.cloudoptic_vpc.id
}


resource "aws_instance" "cloudoptic_instance" {
ami = "ami-abc12345"
instance_type = "t2.micro"
```

```
vpc_security_group_ids = [aws_security_group.cloudoptic_sg.id]

}
```

In this, terraform automatically understands that aws_instance depends on aws_security_group, which in turn depends on aws_vpc. Hence, Terraform will first create the VPC, followed by the security group, and finally the EC2 instance.

Meta-Arguments for Controlling Dependencies

Terraform provides several meta-arguments that offer granular control over dependencies:

- count: Controls how many instances of a resource to create.
- for_each: Allows more complex dependencies with map and set types.
- provisioner: Manages post-creation configurations.

If CloudOptic wants to create multiple EC2 instances but only under specific conditions, the count meta-argument can be utilized.

```
resource "aws_instance" "cloudoptic_instance" {

 count = var.instance_count > 0 ? var.instance_count : 0


 ami = "ami-abc12345"

 instance_type = "t2.micro"

}
```

Here, EC2 instances will only be created if var.instance_count is greater than zero, offering a fine-grained control over resource creation.

Dependency Blocks and Modules

You can declare dependencies between modules in Terraform while utilizing them. Resources inside modules adhere to the dependency order thanks to module-level dependencies.

In the below program, CloudOptic has a module for networking and another for compute resources:

```
module "networking" {
 source = "./modules/networking"
}

module "compute" {
 source = "./modules/compute"

 depends_on = [
 module.networking
 ]
}
```

The compute module will not be initialized until the networking module has been fully applied.

Order of Execution

The order of execution based on dependencies is:

- Resource Creation: Resources with no dependencies are created first.
- Resource Update: Updatable resources are updated in parallel where possible.
- Resource Destruction: Dependent resources are destroyed in the reverse order of creation.

With both explicit and implicit dependencies, and utilizing meta-arguments and modules, you can build highly efficient and reliable infrastructures.

Conditional Attributes

Conditional logic in Terraform is used when you want to make resource provisioning decisions based on variables, resource attributes, or other conditions. It is especially useful in cases where you have to provision resources differently for development, staging, and production environments.

Conditional Operators

Terraform provides a set of conditional operators to implement conditional logic. Some of the basic conditional operators are:

- ==: Equal to
- !=: Not equal to
- >: Greater than
- <: Less than
- >=: Greater than or equal to
- <=: Less than or equal to

Count

One common way to implement conditional logic in Terraform is through the count parameter. Using count, you can decide whether or not to create a resource.

Suppose you want to conditionally create an AWS S3 bucket in CloudOptic based on whether the environment is 'production' or not.

```
variable "environment" {
 default = "development"
}


resource "aws_s3_bucket" "cloudoptic_bucket" {
 count = var.environment == "production" ? 1 : 0
 bucket = "cloudoptic-prod-bucket"
}
```

Here, the S3 bucket will only be created if the environment variable is set to 'production'.

Conditional Expressions

Terraform also supports conditional expressions in the form of:

```
condition ? true_val : false_val
```

If the condition evaluates to true, true_val is returned; otherwise, false_val is returned.

Consider that CloudOptic has different subnets for production and development environments. You could use a conditional expression to choose the subnet.

```
resource "aws_instance" "cloudoptic_instance" {

 subnet_id = var.environment == "production" ? aws_subnet.prod.id : aws_subnet.dev.id

 // Other configurations

}
```

Local Values

You can also use locals to define conditional logic that might be used multiple times throughout your configuration.

Suppose you want to define standard tags for resources but want to include an extra 'Environment' tag for production.

```
locals {

 common_tags = {

 "Owner" = "CloudOptic"

 }



 production_tags = merge(

 local.common_tags,
```

```
{
"Environment" = "Production"
}
)
}

resource "aws_instance" "cloudoptic_instance" {
 tags = var.environment == "production" ? local.production_tags : local.common_tags
 // Other configurations
}
```

In the above code snippet, locals defines a set of common tags and a merged set for production. The appropriate tag set is chosen based on the environment variable.

Conditional Creation and Modules

In a modular architecture, you can use conditions to control the resource provisioning within a module.

If you want to conditionally create a Database cluster in a VPC only for the production environment, the module for this could look like:

```
module "db_cluster" {
 source = "./modules/db_cluster"
 count = var.environment == "production" ? 1 : 0
}
```

This count will be propagated to all resources defined within the db_cluster module.

Dynamic Blocks and Conditional Logic

With Terraform 0.12 and later, dynamic blocks are available to conditionally create nested blocks within resources.

For example, CloudOptic wants to conditionally attach Elastic IPs to EC2 instances:

```
resource "aws_instance" "cloudoptic_instance" {

 // ... other configurations ...



 dynamic "ebs_block_device" {

 for_each = var.environment == "production" ? [1] : []

 content {

 device_name = "/dev/sdh"

 volume_size = 100

 }

 }

}
```

Here, an EBS block device is only attached if the environment is 'production'.

Multiple Conditions with Logical Operators

You can combine conditions using logical operators like && (AND), || (OR), and ! (NOT).

If you want to create an AWS RDS instance only for a production environment and if it's located in the us-west-2 region.

```
resource "aws_db_instance" "cloudoptic_db" {

 count = var.environment == "production" && var.aws_region == "us-west-2" ? 1 : 0

 // Other configurations
```

```
}
```

In the above code snippet, both conditions must be true for the RDS instance to be created.

Conditional Blocks with Dynamic Blocks

Dynamic blocks also support conditions. You can apply conditions within a dynamic block to generate nested blocks conditionally.

Suppose CloudOptic wants to add an IAM role to an EC2 instance only in a production environment.

```
resource "aws_instance" "cloudoptic_instance" {

 // Other configurations



 dynamic "iam_instance_profile" {

 for_each = var.environment == "production" ? [aws_iam_instance_profile.example.name] : []

 content {

 name = iam_instance_profile.value

 }

 }

}
```

Here, the IAM role is attached only if the environment is set to 'production'.

Nested Conditional Statements

You can nest conditional statements to make more complex decisions.

We will assume you want to decide the instance type based on both the environment and whether the instance is GPU-enabled.

```
locals {
 instance_type = var.is_gpu_enabled ? (var.environment == "production" ? "p3.2xlarge" : "p3.large") : "t2.micro"
}

resource "aws_instance" "cloudoptic_instance" {
 instance_type = local.instance_type
 // Other configurations
}
```

Null Values for Optional Attributes

In certain cases, you may want to make an attribute optional based on some condition. The special value null can be useful here.

```
resource "aws_instance" "cloudoptic_instance" {
 key_name = var.environment == "production" ? var.key_name : null
 // Other configurations
}
```

In the above code snippet, key_name will be set only if the environment is 'production'; otherwise, it will be null, effectively making it optional.

All these above conditional logics and attribute methods can make your infrastructure more flexible and adaptable to different scenarios and environments.

Summary

In this chapter, we explored the complex relationship between Terraform properties and conditional logic in an effort to make CloudOptic' infrastructure management more flexible and efficient. To begin, we established the groundwork for more advanced logical operators such as AND, OR, and NOT using simple ternary conditional statements. These operators are significanttools for managing the lifetime of resources in a dynamic environment because they include conditions that govern when a resource should be generated or updated.

Dynamic blocks, which generate layered resource configurations depending on given parameters, provide even more versatility, which we subsequently investigated. When dealing with resources or optional parameters that are environment or configuration specific, these come in handy. The capacity to make complex decisions is further enhanced by nested conditional statements and locals. When we want to choose an AWS instance type depending on the environment and if it has GPU capability, this becomes clear.

This chapter includes covered looping constructs like for_each and for, which help simplify and organize code by conditionally creating many resources from data structures through looping. Lastly, we covered the topic of optional characteristics and how they might be set to null under specific circumstances. Some resource parameters are effectively made optional as a result of this, which has practical ramifications such as only setting an AWS EC2 key name in a production environment.

Test Exercise

1. Ternary Operator Usage: What will the expression count = var.is_production ? 1 : 0 do in a Terraform resource block?
    a. Create the resource only in production
    b. Delete the resource in production
    c. Create the resource regardless of the environment
    d. Throw an error
2. Logical Operators: Which operator is used to evaluate two conditions and returns true if both are true?
    a. AND
    b. OR
    c. NOT
    d. XOR
3. Dynamic Blocks: What is the main advantage of using dynamic blocks?
    a. Error handling
    b. Code Reusability
    c. Nested Looping
    d. Code Efficiency
4. Null Values: What is the purpose of using a null value for an optional attribute?
    a. To generate an error if the attribute is missing
    b. To omit the attribute

    c. To set a default value
    d. To declare an attribute as mandatory
5. Looping Constructs: Which looping method allows for the creation of multiple resources based on keys and values?
    a. for
    b. for_each
    c. while
    d. loop
6. Nested Conditionals: Which of these can be used for more complex decision-making in Terraform?
    a. Locals
    b. Globals
    c. Variables
    d. Constants
7. AWS Instance Type Decision: If you are using nested conditionals to decide the AWS instance type based on environment and GPU support, which Terraform feature would you most likely use?
    a. local
    b. variable
    c. output
    d. data source
8. Optional Attributes: How can you make an attribute optional in a Terraform resource?
    a. Use optional() function
    b. Assign a default value
    c. Use a null value
    d. Make it an output variable
9. AWS EC2 Key Name: If you want to set the AWS EC2 key name only in the production environment, what would you use?
    a. Locals
    b. Ternary Operator
    c. Null Value
    d. Dynamic Block
10. Combining Loops and Conditionals: Which would be the best method to create multiple AWS EC2 instances based on a condition and a list of identifiers?
    a. Using for_each with conditionals
    b. Using for without conditionals
    c. Using count with a static number
    d. Using locals without loops

CHAPTER 6: TERRAFORM MODULES

Introduction to Terraform Modules

Modules, one of Terraform's primary construction blocks, is the primary focus of this chapter. Improving the infrastructure-as-code's scalability and maintainability, modules let you package functionality and resource configurations into reusable blocks. You have the freedom to upgrade or downgrade modules as needed without impacting your primary setup because they can be public or private and there are versions for each.

A common location for sharing modules is the Terraform Registry. You can save a lot of time and energy during development by using pre-built modules that address common use cases. But there are times when prefabricated modules won't cut it; that is when bespoke modules are useful. With custom modules, you may tailor their design to meet the unique requirements of your project, allowing you full command over all of their features and resources.

Modules can be updated with versioning so that they don't interfere with current implementations. To keep your infrastructure consistent with the release of new module versions, you can specify a version number in the module source. An additional safeguard provided by versioning is the ease with which modifications can be rolled back.

The right creation sequence of resources within your module—or even across multiple modules—is ensured by module dependencies. For example, a VPC must be created before an AWS EC2 instance may be created. Most of the time, Terraform manages these dependencies implicitly. However, if your interactions are more complex, you can define them explicitly.

To summarize, this chapter's goal is to offer a thorough grasp of how modules function inside the Terraform ecosystem. It will cover topics such as module types, versioning, the Terraform Registry, and dependency handling. Large infrastructures can be better understood, maintained, and deployed with the help of the modular method, which streamlines management. Because modules may be shared and reused across different projects, it also improves team collaboration.

Deep Dive into Terraform Modules

If resources are the fundamental building blocks of Terraform, then modules are really just containers for many resources. A module is essentially a parameterized artifact that encapsulates a portion of your infrastructure.

Following are some of the most compelling and attractive aspects of terraform modules:

Encapsulation and Abstraction

The first advantage of using modules is the encapsulation of complexity. Imagine a scenario where you are deploying a full-stack application, involving a database, web server, and a load balancer. Each of these components requires various configurations, security settings, and networking rules. Instead of defining all these elements every time you need to set up a new environment, you could encapsulate these settings in a module. The module then exposes only the most critical or variable elements as inputs. This level of abstraction simplifies the interaction with complex setups.

Reusability

Reusability is another compelling aspect of modules. Let us say you have multiple projects that require a Redis cache. Instead of duplicating the same configurations, you can define a 'Redis' module and use it in all of your projects. This practice leads to a 'write once, use many times' methodology, reducing errors, and inconsistencies that could occur when copying and pasting configurations across different projects.

Version Control

Terraform modules can be version-controlled. This feature enables you to iterate on your modules in a controlled manner. If you introduce a new feature or a change in one of your modules, you can version it. Projects that use this module can then choose when to adopt the new version, allowing for staged rollouts and canary testing. This decouples the lifecycle of a module from the projects that use it.

Standardization and Best Practices

Modules can be considered as templates for best practices. For instance, a well-designed module could enforce naming conventions, set up required logging, or configure security settings that comply with an organization's policies. When you distribute a standardized module across multiple teams or projects, you're effectively distributing best practices. This ensures a level of uniformity and compliance that can be very hard to achieve otherwise.

Resource Organization and Management

Modules also help in the logical organization of resources. When your infrastructure grows in complexity, staring at a single main.tf file with hundreds of lines of code becomes overwhelming. Modules allow you to break down this complexity into logical pieces. For example, all your networking-related resources could go into a 'network' module, and all your compute resources could go into a 'compute' module.

Dependency Resolution

Terraform inherently understands the dependencies between resources, but modules allow for more explicit and complex dependency management. For example, a module might depend on outputs from another module. Terraform will ensure that dependent modules are applied only after the modules they depend upon are successfully applied, ensuring a successful orchestration of multiple, complex tasks.

Parameterization

Modules allow for parameterization, which means you can pass in different arguments to alter behavior. For instance, you could have a 'compute' module where the instance type is a variable. For your production environment, you could pass in a high-performance instance type, while in your dev environment, a less expensive instance type could be used.

And, last but not least, there is an active community around Terraform that contributes to a public module registry. This offers modules for common tasks and services, serving as both a resource and inspiration for your projects. Modules are not just a 'nice-to-have'; they're often essential for large-scale IaC.

Types of Modules

Modules in the Terraform ecosystem are classified into several kinds according to their purpose, extent, and interactions with other modules and resources. To better organize and deploy your Terraform settings, it can be helpful to understand the three main categories of modules: Root, Child, and Published.

We will explore these in detail.

Root Modules

Root modules are the entry point in your Terraform configurations. When you run Terraform commands like terraform apply or terraform plan, it's the root module that gets invoked. This module often serves as the orchestrator that calls other modules and ties them together. Essentially, it's the conductor of your infrastructure symphony.

In practical terms, the root module typically resides in the directory where you run your Terraform commands. It uses provider blocks to define which providers are in scope and module blocks to call child modules. Variables and outputs in the root module serve as the primary interface for your Terraform setup, allowing you to parameterize your infrastructure and inspect its state.

Child Modules

Child modules are invoked by other modules, typically root modules, and are not meant to be executed directly. They encapsulate specific functionalities or services, such as a compute instance setup, a database cluster, or a networking configuration.

The real strength of child modules comes from their reusability and abstraction. You can define the complete configuration of a specific AWS S3 bucket in a child module and then invoke that module multiple times from a root module, each time with different input parameters. This is a powerful pattern for enforcing standard configurations across different environments like development, staging, and production.

Published Modules

Published modules are usually generic modules that are designed for public or organization-wide usage. These are hosted on version control systems like Git or are distributed through the Terraform Registry. They are highly parameterized to offer a flexible interface and are usually accompanied by comprehensive documentation.

In essence, published modules are child modules that have been made more generic and robust to be applicable across different scenarios. They follow best practices for security, performance, and availability. Examples include modules for creating Kubernetes clusters, setting up VPCs, or provisioning multi-tier applications.

Additional Module Types

Although less commonly discussed, there are also specialized types of modules based on specific use-cases. For example:

Environment Modules

These are modules specifically tailored to configure an entire environment such as development, staging, or production. They usually wrap around other child modules to create a complete setup.

Meta Modules

These modules don't create any resources themselves but are used to combine multiple child modules into a larger, more complex service.

Data Modules

These are focused solely on fetching and providing data that other modules will use, for example, fetching AMIs or other data sources.

To build a stable, scalable, and maintainable Terraform codebase, each of these module kinds is essential. You can improve the structure of your Terraform projects, make them more reusable, and simplify your infrastructure management operations by learning about their features and optimal uses.

Module Source Options

The place from which a Terraform module will be retrieved is called its source. The extent to which your modules can be reused and shared is heavily dependent on this. This could be your local file system or a remote repository. Terraform gives you a lot of options for how to source modules, and you declare the source using the source argument in a module block. We'll examine these choices and weigh their advantages and disadvantages.

Local Source Paths

Local source paths point to a directory on the same file system where the Terraform configuration is being executed. These are excellent for development and testing but not ideal for sharing or version control.

Example:

```
module "vpc" {

 source = "./modules/vpc"

}
```

GitHub and Git Source

For public and private repositories on GitHub or any other Git-based version control, the URL of the repository can be used as the module source. It's common in organizations that use Git as a code repository. A specific branch, tag, or commit can also be targeted.

Example:

```
module "vpc" {

 source = "git::https://github.com/cloudoptic/terraform-aws-vpc.git?ref=tags/v2.0.0"

}
```

HTTP URLs

Modules can be fetched over HTTP or HTTPS if the server hosts plain .tf files. While this method is versatile, it lacks versioning unless implemented manually on the server.

Example:

```
module "vpc" {

 source = "http://example.com/modules/vpc.tar.gz"

}
```

S3 Buckets

For AWS-centric ecosystems, modules can be hosted on S3 buckets. You can point to a specific version of the module archived as a .tar.gz or .zip file.

Example:

```
module "vpc" {

 source = "s3::https://s3.amazonaws.com/bucket/modules/vpc.tar.gz"

}
```

Terraform Registry

Terraform Registry is a centralized repository for public and private modules. The registry offers an easy-to-use interface, versioning, and a lot of community contributions. You simply specify the organization, module name, and version.

Example:

```
module "vpc" {

 source = "terraform-aws-modules/vpc/aws"

 version = "2.77.0"

}
```

Aside from Git, Terraform also supports Mercurial repositories and Bitbucket as sources, among others. The syntax is similar to that of Git sources.

Imagine you're handling a large-scale infrastructure in CloudOptic. You could store commonly used modules like VPC and EC2 configurations on a secure and version-control Git repository. Your root modules, which might be specific to particular projects or environments, could then source these centralized modules. This ensures standardization and reusability across multiple departments or projects within CloudOptic.

Module Source Best Practices

- Always pin your modules to a specific version or commit to avoid breaking changes.
- If your module source is in a remote repository, it's good practice to document the expected inputs and outputs in the README or similar.
- When sourcing from remote repositories, ensure that proper code reviews are performed, especially for third-party modules.

- Always consider the security implications of where you're sourcing your modules from, especially if sourcing from public repositories. Verify the integrity of the code and consider any potential security vulnerabilities.

Module Inputs and Outputs

When a Terraform configuration calls your module, the inputs and outputs of your module are the main points of contact between the two. Like the parameters and return values of a function in conventional programming, they govern the kind of data that can enter and exit. By providing this abstraction, you can conceal the underlying resource complexity and expose only the information required for the calling configuration. Now we will analyze these important parts.

Module Inputs

Inputs are defined using the variable block within the module's configuration. These variables act as placeholders for actual values that the calling configuration will provide.

Syntax Example:

```
variable "instance_type" {
 type = string
 description = "EC2 instance type"
 default = "t2.micro"
}
```

Using it in a module block:

```
module "ec2_instance" {
 source = "./modules/ec2"
 instance_type = "t3.medium"
}
```

Key Points about Module Inputs

- You can enforce data types like string, number, list, map, or custom object types.
- A default value can be set which will be used if the calling configuration doesn't provide one.
- Always provide descriptions to make it self-explanatory for those who use the module.
- You can also include custom validation rules for your inputs using the validation block.

Module Outputs

Outputs are the data that your module sends back to the calling configuration. They allow you to extract information about the resources created within the module.

Syntax Example:

```
output "instance_public_ip" {

 value = aws_instance.my_instance.public_ip

 description = "The public IP of the instance"

}
```

Accessing it in a calling configuration:

```
output "web_server_ip" {

 value = module.ec2_instance.instance_public_ip

}
```

Key Points about Module Outputs

- Only output information that could be useful for the calling configuration or other dependent modules.
- It's a good habit to include descriptions for your outputs as well.
- Use the sensitive attribute to ensure that sensitive data isn't displayed in logs or the console.

Imagine you have a large infrastructure managed by Terraform in a CloudOptic environment. You could have a VPC module and an EC2 module, each with clearly defined inputs and outputs.

VPC Module Example:

- Inputs: CIDR blocks for public and private subnets, VPC name, tags.
- Outputs: IDs for the VPC, public and private subnets.

EC2 Module Example:

- Inputs: Instance type, key pair name, subnet ID.
- Outputs: Public IP, instance ID, security group IDs.

When you integrate these modules into a bigger Terraform project, you could chain them together based on these inputs and outputs. For instance, the output of the VPC module could serve as an input for the EC2 module, making it an organized, modular, and easily manageable architecture. This would mean that different departments or teams could use these modules as building blocks for their specific projects. The reusability of modules, combined with the clarity of well-defined inputs and outputs, makes it much easier to manage resources at scale. It also improves collaboration as each module can be developed and tested independently before being integrated into the larger ecosystem.

Terraform Variables

Module variables in Terraform are more than just text fields; they are a powerful tool for making modules more customizable, manageable, and user-friendly. They are essential for making your code more reusable and easier to maintain by allowing you to inject modules with adjustable parameters.

We will explore the specific functions of variables in Terraform modules in more detail.

Variables Overview

A Terraform module's variables are essentially a means of encapsulating values that can change with each use of the module. Because of this level of abstraction, the values of the variables can determine how various instances of the same module behave. Although the syntax was covered in the previous section, there is more to the variable block than what meets the eye.

Data Types and Complex Objects

Terraform supports basic types like strings, numbers, and booleans, but you can also define more complex types like lists, sets, maps, and objects. For instance:

```
variable "security_group_rules" {

 type = list(object({
```

```
type = string
from_port = number
to_port = number
protocol = string
cidr_blocks = list(string)
}))
}
```

Here, the security_group_rules variable is a list of objects, each having specific attributes. This flexibility allows you to inject complex configurations into your modules.

Variable Validation

You can ensure the quality and correctness of the input values through validation rules. This is particularly useful when you have strict constraints on what can be passed to the module. For example:

```
variable "instance_type" {
type = string
description = "EC2 instance type"

validation {
condition = contains(["t2.micro", "t2.small", "t3.medium"], var.instance_type)
error_message = "Invalid instance type."
}
}
```

Environmental Variables

Sometimes, you may want to use environmental variables to populate your Terraform variables. Terraform reads environment variables named TF_VAR_name to populate a variable named name. This method can be very useful for injecting secrets or other sensitive information into your configuration in a secure manner.

Module-Specific Role of Variables

Modules use variables as a way to parameterize their operations. Take, as an example, a module that facilitates the creation of an AWS S3 bucket. You can use the name as a variable if each bucket needs to be distinct. To avoid changing the core module code, several configurations might call the module with different names for the bucket.

```
module "s3_bucket" {

 source = "./modules/s3"

 bucket_name = "my_unique_bucket"

}
```

For CloudOptic, where you may be dealing with multi-tenant environments or need to segregate resources based on departments or projects, variables are indispensable. They allow the same module to be used across various use-cases and configurations while maintaining code consistency and reusability.

Variables for Reusability and Versioning

Modules are often versioned to allow progressive enhancements without breaking existing implementations. Variables play a critical role here. As your modules evolve, new features or options can be made available through additional variables or by updating the types or validation rules of existing ones.

Imagine for a moment if you hadn't validated the instance_type variable when you first set it. Adding the validation block to the module, as demonstrated above, would allow you to enforce best practices in the future. Assuming versioning is handled correctly, new setups can take advantage of the validation features while existing ones can keep using the older version of the module.

Think about areas with several collections of resources. Distinct configurations or compliance regulations may apply to these clusters. If you make good use of variables in your Terraform modules, you can adjust to these different requirements without increasing the number of versions of your modules or the amount of code you have to maintain. Using variables, you may construct generic modules and regulate their behavior. This allows them to be used in many scenarios or cluster setups.

Setting Module Version in Terraform

Similar to excellent software versioning, setting module versions in Terraform guarantees that the module behaves consistently and reliably across deployments. This is of the utmost importance in a sophisticated setting such as CloudOptic, where the setup may be lengthy and complicated. The best way to declare and manage module versions is to look into this.

Why Module Versions?

Please understand the significance of module versions before moving on to the practical considerations. The defining modules of your infrastructure are dynamic and adaptable. If versions aren't specified, modifications that haven't been tested yet might be automatically applied, which could lead to unexpected behaviors or configuration errors. Cascade effects that are difficult to diagnose and fix may even occur in large-scale, multi-project settings.

Modules downloaded from the Terraform Registry make version specification a breeze. The registry is a good source for version numbers, which you can use to configure your modules.

We will look at an easy example:

```
module "vpc" {

 source = "terraform-aws-modules/vpc/aws"

 version = "2.64.0"

 // other configurations

}
```

In the above code snippet, Terraform will download and use version 2.64.0 of the VPC module from the Terraform AWS Modules collection. By specifying the version, you ensure that all deployments using this module will behave identically, regardless of when they are executed.

Version Constraints

Terraform allows you to specify version constraints, not just exact versions. This is incredibly useful when you want to ensure that you are using a version that is compatible with your configuration but don't necessarily require an exact version match. For instance:

```
module "vpc" {
 source = "terraform-aws-modules/vpc/aws"
 version = "~> 2.64"
 // other configurations
}
```

In the above code snippet, the version constraint ~> 2.64 implies that any non-breaking updates to version 2.64 are acceptable. This means that 2.65 or 2.66 would work, but 2.63 or 3.0 would not.

Using Local Modules with Versioning

Local modules don't inherently support versioning, but you can mimic this functionality using Git. By placing your local modules in a Git repository, you can use branches, tags, or commit hashes to specify versions.

Consider the following example:

```
module "local_module" {
 source = "git::https://example.com/local_module.git?ref=v1.0.0"
 // other configurations
}
```

Here, the ref=v1.0.0 part specifies that Terraform should use the state of the local_module repository at the tag v1.0.0.

Dynamic Version Pinning

With CloudOptic, you can deal with microservices that share a networking module but have separate configuration needs. For example, in a DevOps pipeline, the networking module can be in a beta state in the development environment and in a stable state in the production environment. The environment can be used to dynamically pin module versions:

```
module "network" {
```

```
source = "git::https://example.com/network_module.git?ref=${var.env == "prod" ? "stable" : "beta"}"

// other configurations

}
```

In the above code snippet, the module version dynamically changes based on the environment, thus allowing more flexibility without compromising stability.

Immutability and Semantic Versioning

Versioning also aligns well with the principle of immutability, ensuring that once a version is published, it does not change. This is often governed by semantic versioning, where versions are labeled in the format of MAJOR.MINOR.PATCH. Each component number is incremented based on the level of change, allowing for more predictable version management.

This could mean different things:

- A MAJOR version change could signify a complete overhaul of how a service is deployed.
- A MINOR change might include new features that don't disrupt existing functionalities.
- A PATCH would be for backward-compatible bug fixes.

By applying these principles, CloudOptic or one can create a robust, scalable, and maintainable infrastructure with a proper versioning strategy that complements its complex requirements.

Exploring Terraform Module Registry

Overview

One place where the community and HashiCorp can store their common configurations and modules is the Terraform Module Registry. Using a module registry can significantly improve efficiency and consistency in a complex system like CloudOptic. It allows configurations to be reused and speeds up the deployment of new services or features.

The Terraform Module Registry is essentially a collection of open-source modules that have been tested and vetted by the community. Each module usually comes with documentation, example usage, and version information, making it easier to understand how to integrate the module into your own configuration. It is a marketplace of sorts but focused on IaC artifacts. It is accessible via a web interface and is searchable, providing a user-friendly way to locate modules for specific cloud providers, services, or tasks.

Basic Navigation and Features

When you first visit the Terraform Module Registry, you'll notice different categories and filters that can help you find what you're looking for. This could be sorted by providers like AWS, Azure, Google Cloud, and more. Each module has its own page, complete with a README, input/output variables, dependencies, and sometimes even guides and examples to get you started. You can sort modules by their popularity, release date, or even look at modules that are verified by HashiCorp, which means they've been specifically tested and supported.

Using Module from Registry

Suppose you need to set up an AWS S3 bucket. Rather than write all the Terraform code from scratch, you can use an existing module from the registry. To do this, you would visit the registry, search for an S3 module, and look at the usage instructions.

Typically, incorporating a module from the registry into your configuration can be as simple as this:

```
module "s3_bucket" {

 source = "terraform-aws-modules/s3-bucket/aws"

 version = "1.8"

 bucket = "my-s3-bucket"

 acl = "private"

}
```

The source indicates the module's location in the registry, and version specifies which version of the module to use. You would then run terraform init to initialize the configuration and download the specified module.

Using Module Outputs

Modules often provide outputs that can be consumed by other parts of your Terraform configuration. For instance, the S3 module might output the bucket ID, which you could use in another module responsible for setting up CloudFront or some other AWS service in your CloudOptic environment. This ensures that the modular components of your infrastructure are not just isolated silos but interact with each other in a cohesive manner.

Forking and Customizing Modules

While the registry offers a plethora of options, there may be times when you need to modify a module to better suit your CloudOptic-specific requirements. In such cases, you can fork the module repository, make your changes, and then point to your custom repository as the module source. This ensures that your custom needs are met without reinventing the wheel.

Private Module Registry

A private module registry is an option in Terraform Cloud and Terraform Enterprise, which could be useful for enterprises like CloudOptic that need to manage a set of internal, reusable modules. This comes in handy when you have modules that contain logic exclusive to your business or sensitive data that shouldn't be made public.

Versioning and the Registry

The Registry also allows you to browse through different versions of a module, making it simpler to find a version that suits your needs or to upgrade to a newer version in a controlled manner. This is critical for ensuring that your infrastructure remains as stable and predictable as possible.

Auditing and Security Concerns

It's important to vet the modules you intend to use. Even though modules from the Terraform Registry are often well-documented and vetted by the community, security audits are crucial, especially for environments with specific compliance requirements of CloudOptic.

Creating Custom Modules

Need for Custom Modules

Although there are many pre-built, community-supported modules available in the Terraform Module Registry, there are times when a more tailored solution is required. One of the many uses for custom modules is to encapsulate one-of-a-kind business logic, facilitate integration with proprietary software, or satisfy particular security and compliance requirements that generic modules might miss. Custom modules provide platform-specific solutions for managing services or workflows, making them ideal for specialized ecosystems like CloudOptic.

Advantages of Custom Modules

- Custom modules can encapsulate internal best practices or configurations unique to your organization.
- Having a custom module means you can maintain its versioning, keeping historical changes and updates well-organized.

- Custom modules can be shared internally within the team or across multiple projects, providing a consistent approach to problem-solving.

Groundwork for Custom Module

It is critical to establish the directory structure before beginning to construct the custom module. As an example, imagine you're interested in managing an AWS S3 bucket for CloudOptic, but you'd like to add some custom logging and notification capabilities.

An example of the directory's layout would be:

```
cloudoptic_s3_module/
│
├── main.tf
├── variables.tf
├── outputs.tf
```

main.tf

This is where the main configuration will reside. The AWS S3 bucket can be created as follows:

```
provider "aws" {
 region = "us-west-2"
}


resource "aws_s3_bucket" "cloudoptic_bucket" {
 bucket = var.bucket_name
 acl = "private"


 server_side_encryption_configuration {
```

```
rule {
apply_server_side_encryption_by_default {
sse_algorithm = "AES256"
}
}
}

dynamic "logging" {
for_each = var.enable_logging ? [1] : []
content {
target_bucket = aws_s3_bucket.log_bucket.bucket
target_prefix = "log/"
}
}
}
```

variables.tf

Here, you'll define all the input variables for the module:

```
variable "bucket_name" {
description = "The name of the bucket"
type = string
}
```

```
variable "enable_logging" {
 description = "Enable bucket logging"
 type = bool
 default = false
}
```

outputs.tf

Lastly, you'll expose some outputs for the module:

```
output "bucket_id" {
 value = aws_s3_bucket.cloudoptic_bucket.id
}


output "bucket_arn" {
 value = aws_s3_bucket.cloudoptic_bucket.arn
}
```

Using Custom Module

To use this module in a CloudOptic project, you could have a configuration like the following:

```
module "cloudoptic_s3" {
 source = "./cloudoptic_s3_module"
 bucket_name = "my-co-bucket"
```

```
enable_logging = true
}
```

Here, source points to the local directory containing the custom module. bucket_name and enable_logging are input variables.

When designing a custom module for CloudOptic, it's good to make it as parameterized as possible. The use of variables like enable_logging allows you to make the module more flexible and adaptable to different requirements within CloudOptic.

One essential aspect when creating a custom module, especially for a security-centric platform like CloudOptic, is ensuring that it adheres to the organization's compliance and security requirements. The module should be reviewed and tested rigorously before making it a part of the infrastructure.

Managing Module Dependencies

Module dependencies in Terraform can be tricky yet powerful. Managing dependencies ensures that resources are created in the correct order, and it establishes relationships between modules. When your infrastructure's complexity grows, being skilled in dependency management becomes crucial.

Dependency Blocks within Modules

Within a module block, you can also use the depends_on attribute to specify the module's dependencies. This method shines when, inside a module, you have a collection of resources that rely on each other.

Consider that cloudoptic_monitoring and cloudoptic_logging are two modules. The monitoring module is necessary for the logging module to function. Below is an example of how the usage would appear:

```
module "cloudoptic_monitoring" {
 source = "./cloudoptic_monitoring"
 // variables here
}
```

```
module "cloudoptic_logging" {
 source = "./cloudoptic_logging"
 // variables here


 depends_on = [module.cloudoptic_monitoring]
}
```

Data Blocks and Dependency

Data blocks often require explicit dependency management. Because data blocks fetch data that must be available before creating resources, they often need to depend on the completion of certain tasks or the creation of certain resources. For example:

```
data "aws_instance" "example" {
 depends_on = [aws_instance.my_instance]


 filter {
 name = "tag:Name"
 values = [aws_instance.my_instance.tags["Name"]]
 }
}
```

Conditional Dependencies

Sometimes dependencies are conditional, meaning they only apply under certain conditions. For instance, you may have optional modules that are only invoked based on a Boolean variable. In such cases, you'll need to conditionally set dependencies to ensure proper resource creation order.

Following is an example:

```
module "cloudoptic_optional_feature" {
  count = var.enable_feature ? 1 : 0
  // variables here
}

module "cloudoptic_main" {
  // variables here
  depends_on = var.enable_feature ? [module.cloudoptic_optional_feature] : []
}
```

In the above code snippet, the cloudoptic_main module will only depend on cloudoptic_optional_feature if enable_feature is set to true.

Nested Module Dependencies

Complex projects often involve nested modules, where one module calls another. Managing dependencies in such a layered structure requires careful consideration. If a child module depends on a resource in the parent module, you have to propagate this dependency explicitly.

```
module "cloudoptic_child" {
  source = "./cloudoptic_child"
  // variables here


  depends_on = [aws_s3_bucket.parent_bucket]
}
```

Dependency Locking with Version Constraints

Modules can be versioned, and Terraform can fetch the appropriate versions as needed. This is particularly important for managing dependencies because it ensures that your modules will behave as expected even when updates are made to dependent modules. You can set version constraints in the module block to lock dependencies to a particular version:

```
module "cloudoptic_logging" {

 source = "app.terraform.io/example/logging/aws"

 version = "1.0.4"

}
```

There are pros and cons to dependency management. Dependencies facilitate orderly, modular, and reusable code, but they can provide complexity and possible difficulties if not handled properly. You may significantly improve the stability and maintainability of your Terraform projects by learning the ins and outs of dependencies (both explicit and implicit), becoming an expert with depends_on, thinking about conditionals, and using version restrictions.

Summary

This chapter went into long detail about how to manage module dependencies in Terraform, which is a key part of planning how tools and modules work together and in what order. Both implicit and explicit dependencies were clarified. With Terraform's auto-detected implicit dependencies, even the most basic relationships are no longer an unknown. When dealing with non-configurable items, such as API readiness, or more complicated interactions, the depends_on property is necessary for explicit dependencies.

Conditional dependencies, dependency propagation in nested modules, and other advanced subjects were presented during the learnings of explicit dependencies. One way to create a dependency chain with conditions is to use variables to activate modules on a case-by-case basis. When working with nested modules, it is necessary to explicitly state the relationship between child and parent modules when using resources. This allows Terraform to manage resources efficiently. When working in specialized contexts, such as CloudOptic, this becomes even more crucial.

Data blocks, which frequently necessitate clear dependencies, were additionally investigated. When the dependence property is required because data must be obtained before any resource can be created, these become very important. Lastly, the chapter explored dependency locking, a method of versioning that is crucial for ensuring a predictable and stable infrastructure. This becomes even more important when using third-party modules or services like Terraform

Registry.

Managing dependencies in a modular Terraform project is more complicated than you may think. You will become an expert IaC practitioner and have stronger Terraform scripts if you know when to employ explicit or implicit dependencies, how to use conditionals, and the significance of version locking.

Test Exercise

1. What are implicit dependencies?
    a. Dependencies declared using depends_on
    b. Dependencies automatically detected by Terraform
    c. Dependencies between sibling modules
    d. None of the above
2. How would you create an explicit dependency?
    a. Using depends_on attribute
    b. It's auto-detected, no need to specify
    c. Using the source attribute
    d. By placing modules in the same directory
3. What is dependency propagation in nested modules?
    a. Auto detection of dependencies in parent modules
    b. Child modules inheriting dependencies from parent modules
    c. Parent modules inheriting dependencies from child modules
    d. Random allocation of dependencies in nested modules
4. How can conditional dependencies be crafted?
    a. Using loops
    b. Using variables
    c. By manually configuring each resource
    d. Not possible in Terraform
5. What is the main purpose of dependency locking?
    a. To allow automatic updates
    b. To freeze the version of dependencies for stability
    c. To introduce breaking changes
    d. To increase resource provisioning speed
6. When are data blocks used in the context of dependencies?
    a. When resources require data to be fetched beforehand
    b. When data is part of an output block
    c. When there is a cyclic dependency
    d. When implicit dependency is not possible
7. What should you consider when declaring explicit dependencies for nested modules?
    a. Making sure all modules are published to the Terraform Registry

    b. Using the depends_on attribute in the child module only
    c. Declaring dependencies both in parent and child modules
    d. The sequence of modules in the main configuration file
8. In CloudOptic, how important is versioning in dependency management?
    a. Not important, CloudOptic auto-manages versions
    b. Crucial for ensuring a stable and predictable environment
    c. Important only for the initial setup
    d. Irrelevant, as CloudOptic doesn't support versioning
9. How are explicit dependencies typically used in specialized environments like CloudOptic?
    a. To manage inter-module communication
    b. To manage API readiness and service provisioning
    c. To manage variables and outputs
    d. To manage logging and monitoring
10. Which kind of dependency is usually needed for non-configurable elements like API readiness?
    a. Implicit
    b. Explicit
    c. Conditional
    d. Cyclic

CHAPTER 7: TERRAFORM IMPORT AND MAINTENANCE

Overview

In this chapter, we will delve into many advanced Terraform issues that are essential for infrastructure management, particularly for a firm like CloudOptic that may require complicated and scalable solutions.

It comprises:

- Terraform Import: Terraform import allows you to bring already provisioned resources under Terraform management. This feature is particularly useful when you have an existing infrastructure and wish to manage it using Terraform going forward.
- Purpose and Usage: The main purpose is to ease the transition between manual infrastructure management and IaC. By using Terraform import, you ensure that existing settings or data aren't overwritten, making it a safer approach for companies like CloudOptic.
- Ideal Maintenance Strategy for CloudOptic: For a cloud solutions company like CloudOptic, a hybrid approach could be ideal, which combines automated monitoring and manual checks. Tools like Terraform can be used to codify infrastructure needs, while manual reviews can serve as a last line of defense.
- Resource Targeting: Resource targeting allows you to apply actions like create, update, or destroy to specific resources rather than an entire stack. This is very useful in microservices architectures or in modular infrastructures where you don't want a change in one module to affect the others.
- State Manipulation Commands: These commands allow you to manually intervene in the lifecycle of your resources. They are crucial for debugging or when you're looking to make minor changes without affecting the entire infrastructure.
- Updating Terraform Codebases: Keeping your Terraform code up to date is vital. This involves updating to newer versions of Terraform, cleaning deprecated features, and integrating any new best practices. It's an ongoing process that is part of the CI/CD pipeline in most modern enterprises, including CloudOptic.

All of these things are fundamental to advanced Terraform administration, particularly in settings that demand adaptability, scalability, and dependability—just like CloudOptic. As we move further in this chapter, we will explore each of these subjects in more detail.

Terraform Import and Its Utilization

You can put infrastructure resources that are already in place or that are handled manually under Terraform control using the Terraform import capability, which is a fundamental part of Terraform. For many businesses, this is an essential first step in making the switch to the more automated Infrastructure-as-Code (IaC) paradigm for infrastructure management. As a component of Terraform's ecosystem, the tool is an essential part of any contemporary cloud management strategy.

Importance of Terraform Import

- Imagine you've gone to the trouble of manually configuring multiple AWS instances and have finally decided to use Terraform for their management. Connecting these instances to your IaC models is made easy using the terraform import command. By avoiding the need to recreate these resources specifically for your Terraform operation, you can save time.
- Established businesses may have relied on scripts or manual setup for their initial infrastructure. The import command is going to be really helpful when they decide to switch to an IaC paradigm.
- Terraform allows for the codification and versioning of resource configurations upon import. That way, you can rest assured that everyone is following company policy and that audits will be a breeze. This is particularly helpful because CloudOptic is probably dealing with complicated regulatory standards.
- Terraform settings make it easy to manage, modify, or delete resources after import. Because of this, tactics for optimizing resources like labeling, scalability, and automated backups can be implemented.
- Team members can better grasp the infrastructure's status and configuration after importing resources into a Terraform state file. They may make the process more collaborative by pulling this state file to their local environments, making modifications, and pushing updates.
- You may simplify your disaster recovery procedure by bringing everything under Terraform. If the entire infrastructure is defined, then it's much easier to replace it after a catastrophic collapse.
- Depending on the situation, businesses such as CloudOptic may work with hybrid or multiple cloud platforms. When dealing with such dispersed and varied materials, terraform import can be useful for managing everything from a single interface.

The Mechanics of Import

The basic syntax of terraform import is straightforward:

```
terraform import [options] ADDRESS ID
```

- ADDRESS: The address of the Terraform resource to import.

- ID: The specific ID Terraform will assign to the resource, which typically corresponds to the native cloud service identifier.

Below is a basic example for importing an AWS EC2 instance:

```
terraform import aws_instance.my_instance i-1234567890abcdef0
```

In this example, aws_instance.my_instance is the address that corresponds to a resource block in a Terraform configuration file. i-1234567890abcdef0 is the AWS EC2 instance ID.

After running the import command, Terraform will import the current state of the resource and produce a state file that you can then manage with Terraform. You must ensure that the Terraform configuration files have a corresponding resource block for each imported resource, or else Terraform will plan to delete the resources during the next application because they are not in the configuration.

Challenges and Caveats

While terraform import is undoubtedly powerful, it's not a silver bullet. It imports only the resource's state, not its configuration. You must still write the configuration code that aligns with that state. Additionally, not all Terraform providers support import, and some might have restrictions on what can be imported.

Sample Program: Terraform Import for Complex Resources

Consider that CloudOptic has a sophisticated AWS configuration that consists of an S3 container for data storage and a VPC (Virtual Private Cloud) containing multiple EC2 instances. The primary goal here is to get these assets into a Terraform setup.

Pre-requisites

- Terraform installed
- AWS CLI installed and configured
- AWS resources manually created or managed by other means

Setup Configuration Blocks

Before running terraform import, you'll need a Terraform configuration that aligns with the resources you're importing. Create a main.tf file with placeholders for the resources.

Following is a skeletal configuration:

```
provider "aws" {
 region = "us-west-2"
}

resource "aws_vpc" "imported_vpc" {
}

resource "aws_instance" "imported_instance" {
}

resource "aws_s3_bucket" "imported_bucket" {
}
```

Importing the Resources

First, we import an existing VPC. Use AWS CLI to find the VPC ID.

```
aws ec2 describe-vpcs
```

Then import it:

```
terraform import aws_vpc.imported_vpc vpc-0abcd1234efgh5678
```

Use AWS CLI to find EC2 instance IDs.

```
aws ec2 describe-instances
```

Import the instance:

```
terraform import aws_instance.imported_instance i-1234567890abcdef0
```

Use AWS CLI to find your bucket name.

```
aws s3api list-buckets
```

Then import the bucket:

```
terraform import aws_s3_bucket.imported_bucket my-bucket-name
```

After importing, you'll have a terraform.tfstate file that contains the current state of your imported resources. However, the main.tf only has placeholders. You have to fill these in manually. Use the terraform show command to display the imported state, then align your main.tf configuration with this state.

For example, if the imported EC2 instance is of type t2.micro, your configuration block would look like:

```
resource "aws_instance" "imported_instance" {

 instance_type = "t2.micro"

 ami = "ami-0abcd1234efgh5678"

 // other required attributes

}
```

Configuration Importer Tools

The terraform import command does not automatically generate configuration. However, third-party tools like terraformer can help in importing both state and configuration, although they come with their caveats and might not always be up-to-date with the latest Terraform providers. These tools scan your cloud environment and generate .tf configuration files in addition to importing the state.

To use terraformer for AWS:

```
terraformer import aws --resources="vpc,instances,s3" --regions=us-west-2 --profile=default
```

This command will import VPCs, EC2 instances, and S3 buckets from the us-west-2 region using the default AWS CLI profile. terraformer will generate .tf files corresponding to these resources.

Beware of Drift

Once you've imported existing resources into Terraform, be cautious of "configuration drift," where the state file and actual resource configurations can diverge. Utilize tools like terraform plan to regularly check for drift and rectify any discrepancies.

Managing Configuration Drift

Every team faces the challenge of configuration drift when it comes to managing IaC. When this happens, it's because the infrastructure's real condition is different from what your Terraform configurations are describing.

We can find out how to handle this kind of drift if we look into it.

Detecting Configuration Drift

The primary command to detect drift in Terraform is terraform plan. This command will compare the last-known state (stored in terraform.tfstate) with the current real-world infrastructure. A terraform plan execution will identify any differences between your state and the live infrastructure.

```
terraform plan
```

This command will provide a detailed report. Resources that are in sync will show no changes, while those with drift will be marked for modifications (~) or destruction (-).

Managing Drift

Terraform 0.15 and later versions have introduced the terraform plan -refresh-only command. This is solely designed to update the state file with real-world infrastructure details without making any changes. This is especially useful for just detecting drift.

```
terraform plan -refresh-only
```

The above command only refreshes the state to match real-world infrastructure but doesn't change the infrastructure. After that, you can decide how to reconcile the drift.

Reconcile Drift

The simplest way to reconcile drift is by running a terraform apply. This will align the real-world resources with the Terraform configuration.

```
terraform apply
```

Just a heads up, this will make the infrastructure conform to the Terraform files, which might be a problem if the drift wasn't intended.

Manual Reconciliation

If you find that the drift was intentional (perhaps an emergency scaling operation that had to bypass Terraform), you'll need to manually update your Terraform configurations to reflect this new intended state.

For instance, let's say someone manually scaled an EC2 instance from t2.micro to t2.small. Your Terraform configuration for this instance might look like:

```
resource "aws_instance" "example_instance" {

 instance_type = "t2.micro"

 ami = "ami-0abcd1234efgh5678"

}
```

After discovering the drift, you should update it to:

```
resource "aws_instance" "example_instance" {

 instance_type = "t2.small"

 ami = "ami-0abcd1234efgh5678"

}
```

Then run terraform apply to ensure the new state is saved without making any changes to the real-world resources.

Drift Detection Tools

While terraform plan and terraform apply can address drift, sometimes, you need an automated way to detect and alert on drift, especially for large infrastructures like that at CloudOptic as below:

- Cloud Custodian: This tool can be configured to scan AWS resources and notify if they don't meet specified conditions. It can be integrated into a CI/CD pipeline for regular drift checks.
- AWS Config: If you're on AWS, AWS Config can track changes to resources and notify you when drift occurs.
- Custom Scripts: You can write custom scripts that use cloud provider APIs to check the state of resources and compare them against a Terraform state file or another desired state representation.

These automated tools can be particularly useful for organizations like CloudOptic where the scale of the infrastructure can make manual checks impractical. You could, for example, integrate these tools into your CI/CD pipeline to run checks after every deployment or on a schedule. This helps in maintaining an accurate Terraform state and minimizing the risks associated with configuration drift.

Terraform Resource Targeting

If you run a complicated infrastructure as CloudOptic does, you need Terraform's resource targeting functionality. When it comes to state management, partial deployments, and debugging, the ability to target certain resources can be incredibly helpful. Terraform gives you more control over infrastructure modifications by letting you designate which resources are subject to its three operations: apply, plan, and destroy.

Syntax for Resource Targeting

Resource targeting is typically done using the -target flag followed by the resource type and name. The basic syntax is as follows:

```
terraform apply -target=resource_type.resource_name
```

Use Cases for Resource Targeting

Selective Updates

Imagine you have multiple EC2 instances and only one needs an update. Instead of applying the update to all, you can target just the one in question.

```
terraform apply -target=aws_instance.my_specific_instance
```

Dependent Resource Modification

Suppose you have a VPC, and within it, you have a security group. If you need to modify just the security group, you can specifically target it.

```
terraform apply -target=aws_security_group.my_security_group
```

Debugging

If you are troubleshooting an issue with a specific resource, targeting allows you to isolate Terraform operations to just that one, making it easier to identify issues without affecting other resources.

Targeting with Resource Addressing

You can be more specific with your targeting by utilizing resource addressing. For example, you can target a specific instance within a resource block that uses count or for_each to create multiple instances.

```
terraform apply -target=aws_instance.my_instances[0]
```

Targeting Multiple Resources

You can also specify multiple targets in a single command by appending additional -target flags:

```
terraform apply -target=aws_instance.instance_one -target=aws_security_group.sg_one
```

Terraform will still evaluate dependencies, even if you've targeted a specific resource. If you modify a resource that other resources depend on, those will be updated as well. Since targeting allows you to operate on a subset of resources, there is a risk of ending up with a state file that doesn't match the actual infrastructure if you're not careful.

Automating Resource Targeting in CI/CD

Your CI/CD pipeline scripts can be configured to target specific resources, since CloudOptic probably uses CI/CD for infrastructure installations. As an example, consider a Jenkins pipeline that incorporates a terraform apply command with resource targeting as one of its steps.

```
pipeline {
 agent any
 stages {
 stage('Targeted Terraform Apply') {
 steps {
 sh '''
 terraform init
 terraform apply -target=aws_instance.my_specific_instance -auto-approve
 '''
 }
 }
 }
}
```

This stage could be triggered only under specific conditions or as part of a broader pipeline that includes tests, code reviews, and so on.

Overall, the -target flag offers flexibility for partial deployments and troubleshooting, but it should be used judiciously to ensure that the Terraform state and the infrastructure stay in sync.

Terraform State Manipulation Commands

Part of managing your infrastructure in Terraform is mastering state manipulation. Whether you're dealing with CloudOptic or any other circumstance, it's essential for keeping your configuration files up-to-date with real-world resources.

In this section, we'll delve into the available commands to manipulate state files.

terraform state list

The terraform state list command is used to list resources within a Terraform state file. When executed, this command displays all resources and their statuses.

```
terraform state list
```

terraform state show

This command is for inspecting a single resource in the state file in detail. It provides more information than the list command.

```
terraform state show aws_instance.my_instance
```

terraform state mv

This command is designed to move items within a state file or even to a completely different state file. This is useful when you're refactoring your Terraform configurations and need to align the state file accordingly.

```
terraform state mv aws_instance.old aws_instance.new
```

You can also use it to move a resource to a different state file entirely, maybe as part of a state file segregation strategy:

```
terraform state mv -state-out="new.tfstate" aws_instance.my_instance aws_instance.my_instance
```

terraform state rm

This command is used to remove items from a state file. Ensure that this doesn't destroy the actual resource; it merely unlinks it from the state file. This could be useful for detaching a manually managed resource from Terraform management.

```
terraform state rm aws_instance.unwanted
```

terraform state pull

The terraform state pull command is employed to manually download and output the state from remote backends. This can be useful for debugging or when you need to manipulate the state file locally.

```
terraform state pull > my-local-state.tfstate
```

terraform state push

This is the opposite of pull. It uploads a local state file to a remote backend. However, it's a risky operation and should be used cautiously.

```
terraform state push my-local-state.tfstate
```

terraform state replace-provider

In cases where you're migrating from one provider version to another or from one provider to a completely different one, the terraform state replace-provider command can be invaluable.

```
terraform state replace-provider hashicorp/aws registry.internal.corp/aws
```

State File Backup in CI/CD

It would be quite beneficial for CloudOptic to incorporate state modification commands into their CI/CD pipeline, assuming it does so. As a precaution, a Jenkins job could, for instance, fetch the current state prior to implementing any modifications:

```
pipeline {
 agent any
 stages {
 stage('Backup State File') {
 steps {
 sh '''
 terraform state pull > backup.tfstate
 '''
```

```
}
}
}
}
```

Limitations and Precautions

- Commands like terraform state rm and terraform state mv have the potential to make irreversible changes.
- Be cautious with pull and push operations, especially when multiple team members or automated processes are interacting with the same state file.
- Ensure the state file version is compatible with the Terraform version you're using. Incompatibility can lead to corruption or misinterpretation of the state.

In essence, Terraform state manipulation commands grant you substantial control over your state files, allowing for detailed inspection, modification, and backup. These tools are particularly vital for maintaining state integrity and should be an integral part of any advanced Terraform usage strategy, including that of CloudOptic.

Updating Terraform Codebase

Maintaining an up-to-date Terraform codebase is similar to scheduling routine auto maintenance: it's annoying, but it's necessary for the car's performance and health in the long run. Security holes and incompatibilities with new features are only two of the many problems that might arise from a codebase that is too old. Running into these problems can cause major delays and extra expenses, especially for a company which operates at an enterprise level.

Conceptual Importance

Security holes and incompatibility with new features are just two of the many problems that can arise from not updating the Terraform source. These concerns, in particular, can cause large delays and higher expenses, especially for companies. Avoiding operational hazards isn't the only reason it's important to maintain the codebase current.

Priority number one is security, since older providers and modules may have security flaws that have been fixed in later versions. Improved performance, usability, and resource efficiency are only a few outcomes of the ongoing evolution of the Terraform ecosystem. Deprecation of functionality or even whole versions of providers is another important consideration; failing to apply updates on a regular basis could render your infrastructure unsupported. By keeping the codebase up-to-date, teams working on the same projects are able to collaborate more effectively and experience fewer disagreements.

An updated Terraform codebase is crucial for enterprises, especially those in regulated industries, to meet the non-negotiable requirement of complying with numerous standards. The many advantages of keeping the Terraform codebase current are highlighted by the fact that newer versions often contain performance improvements. These changes help speed up execution times and reduce cloud-related expenses.

Sample Program: Keeping Codebase Updated

Take, for example, CloudOptic' use of Terraform to oversee an intricate AWS infrastructure that comprises EC2 instances, RDS databases, and a host of other AWS services.

This is how you can ensure that your Terraform codebase is always up-to-date:

Version Pinning

Start by pinning the versions of providers and modules. While this may seem counterintuitive, it actually gives you control over updates.

```
provider "aws" {

 version = "~> 2.0"

}
```

In this example, CloudOptic is ensuring that it uses the AWS provider's 2.x versions.

Regular Checks and Audits

Utilize automated checks, perhaps as part of your CI/CD pipeline, to inform you of outdated versions of providers and modules. Tools like tfsec or checkov can assist in this.

```
checkov -d .
```

Manual Review

Before upgrading, always read the release notes and migration guides. This is crucial for understanding what has changed, what new features have been introduced, and what bugs have been fixed.

Test Environment

Always test updates in a non-production environment first. This can be done using Terraform workspaces or by maintaining separate state files for different environments.

```
terraform workspace new test

terraform apply
```

Gradual Rollout

Once testing is complete, roll out the updates incrementally. You could first update non-critical resources and monitor them before updating critical resources.

For CloudOptic, which likely deals with a large, dynamic infrastructure, automating these steps through scripts or CI/CD pipelines can save time and reduce errors.

```
pipeline {

 agent any

 stages {

 stage('Check for Updates') {

 steps {

 sh '''

 terraform init

 terraform providers schema -json > current-providers.json

 check-for-updates current-providers.json // Custom script to check for updates

 '''

 }

 }

 }
```

}

Monitoring and Alerting

Post-update, monitor the infrastructure to ensure that everything is working as expected. If something does go wrong, the earlier backup procedures can be a lifesaver.

Following these suggestions will help CloudOptic keep its Terraform codebase secure, efficient, and current, which will lower the risk of infrastructure management. If you want your operations to be scalable and safe, you need to ensure that your codebase is updated.

Summary

We covered a lot of ground in this chapter about how to keep a Terraform environment running well, with an emphasis on how to import Terraform, manage configuration drift, target resources, manipulate states, and keep the Terraform codebase updated—all of which are important for a large-scale company like CloudOptic. A potent method for bringing resources that are already in existence or are managed manually under the control of Terraform is the Terraform import. Importing the state is easy, but writing the configuration by hand could be a pain for complicated resources, as we discovered.

Another important issue was configuration drift, which occurs when the status of the resources in the actual world differs from the state of the resources in the Terraform state file. We emphasized the significance of being disciplined when making changes to infrastructure by exploring the terraform refresh and terraform apply commands to detect and fix drift. When working with large-scale infrastructures, the ability to precisely target resources makes it possible to make surgical modifications to such resources. But it has a flip side: configuration drift might occur if not handled properly.

We also learned how to manage state files using commands like terraform state rm and terraform state mv, among others. These instructions provide a fine-grained level of control, which is very helpful in complicated and dynamic infrastructures. For many reasons, including security and the availability of new features, it is critical to maintain the Terraform codebase updated. We went over best practices that CloudOptic may use to keep their codebase secure and robust, and we learnd them through a method to conduct upgrades in a controlled and monitored way.

Test Exercise

1. What is the primary purpose of Terraform import?
    a. To destroy existing resources
    b. To bring existing resources under Terraform management

    c. To update the Terraform codebase
    d. To backup the Terraform state file
2. Which command is used to correct configuration drift in Terraform?
    a. terraform destroy
    b. terraform init
    c. terraform refresh
    d. terraform plan
3. What does resource targeting enable?
    a. Deleting specific resources
    b. Updating only selected resources
    c. Creating new resources only
    d. Deleting the entire infrastructure
4. Which state manipulation command is used to rename or move resources?
    a. terraform state rm
    b. terraform state mv
    c. terraform state list
    d. terraform state import
5. Why is it important to keep the Terraform codebase updated?
    a. It's not necessary
    b. To leverage new features
    c. To reduce cost
    d. To make it more complex
6. How is configuration drift usually discovered?
    a. After running terraform init
    b. After running terraform apply
    c. After running terraform destroy
    d. After running terraform refresh
7. What's the primary risk associated with resource targeting?
    a. It is time-consuming
    b. It can cause configuration drift
    c. It can corrupt the state file
    d. It can remove all resources
8. What is the limitation of terraform import for complex resources?
    a. It cannot import the state
    b. It cannot import the configuration
    c. It cannot handle more than 10 resources
    d. It can import only in JSON format
9. Which command is NOT a state manipulation command?
    a. terraform state mv
    b. terraform state show
    c. terraform state backup
    d. terraform apply

10. What's a prudent step before updating the Terraform codebase?
    a. Perform a backup of the current state
    b. Delete all resources
    c. Rename the configuration files
    d. Update all modules to the latest version without testing

CHAPTER 8: BEST PRACTICES AND DESIGN PATTERNS

Introduction to Advanced Terraform Practices

This chapter will cover several aspects of best practices that can significantly improve your Terraform usage. This comprises:

- Style Guide: The suggested style and structural patterns that improve code readability and maintainability are covered in the Terraform Style Guide.
- Reusable Modules: Discover how to write modules that can be applied to several projects at once, significantly minimizing errors and code duplication.
- Environment Isolation: To reduce risk and make testing easier, this section will go into detail on how to isolate various environments, such as development, staging, and production.
- Scalability and Performance: How can you ensure your Terraform setups can grow as your projects do? We'll look at optimization strategies to improve performance and scalability.
- Best Practices: Although there are many ways to use terraform, some methods are demonstrably more efficient, safe, and effective than others. This will be an assortment of these procedures targeted at an organization with requirements like CloudOptic.

Anyone taking IaC seriously, especially in a dynamic setting, must pay close attention to these topics. The forthcoming sections will cover each part in long detail, helping us to both comprehend the theory and put these best practices into practice.

Terraform Style Guide and Best Practices

Coding in Terraform according to a style guide is about more than simply looking good; it's also about making the code more readable, maintainable, and error-free. Having the correct standards in place may transform a project from a delight to a misery.

We will look into the essential components of a Terraform style guide and illustrate them with our ongoing CloudOptic example.

Formatting Conventions

Indentation

Use two spaces for indentation. Terraform has its own formatter that can be triggered with terraform fmt to ensure your code follows this rule.

```
resource "aws_instance" "example" {
```

```
 ami = "ami-0c55b159cbfafe1f0"

 instance_type = "t2.micro"

}
```

Naming Conventions

Stick to snake_case for filenames and identifiers, such as variable names, resource names, and outputs. Keep names descriptive yet succinct.

```
variable "instance_count" {

 description = "Number of instances to create"

 default = 1

}
```

Comments and Documentation

Use # for single-line comments and /* ... */ for multi-line comments. Always document variables and outputs; for complex modules or resources, inline comments are crucial.

```
# This output is used to retrieve the instance ID

output "instance_id" {

 value = aws_instance.example.id

}
```

Resource Blocks

Declare resources with required arguments first, followed by optional arguments. Keep the ordering consistent across your codebase.

```
resource "aws_instance" "example" {

 # Required
```

```
ami = "ami-0c55b159cbfafe1f0"

instance_type = "t2.micro"


# Optional

key_name = var.key_name

}
```

Variables and Outputs

Always describe what each variable is used for and what each output represents. This makes your code self-explanatory.

```
variable "subnet_id" {

description = "The ID of the VPC Subnet"

}
```

Modules

When calling modules, use named arguments instead of positional arguments. This makes it clear what each argument represents.

```
module "vpc" {

source = "./modules/vpc"

cidr_block = "10.0.0.0/16"

}
```

Sample Program: Using Style Principles

To better illustrate these style principles, we will modify an example codebase of CloudOptic Terraform.

Initial Code:

```
resource "aws_s3_bucket" "b" {bucket="my-tf-test-bucket"acl="private"}
```

After applying style guide:

```
# CloudOptic S3 Bucket

resource "aws_s3_bucket" "cloudoptic_bucket" {

 # Required arguments

 bucket = "cloudoptic-my-tf-test-bucket"

 acl = "private"


 # Optional arguments

 tags = {

 Environment = "Dev"

 ManagedBy = "Terraform"

 }

}
```

In the above sample program, the code is reformatted for better readability. We added a meaningful name for the S3 bucket, following the snake_case naming convention. Required and optional arguments are separated, and inline comments were added for clarity.

Strategic Purpose of Variables and Locals

Variables help in parameterizing the Terraform configurations, thus making it reusable.

```
variable "region" {
```

```
description = "AWS region to deploy resources in"
default = "us-west-2"
}
```

Locals can be used for setting default values or composing multiple variables.

```
locals {
 default_tags = {
 ManagedBy = "Terraform"
 Environment = "Dev"
 }
}
```

Leveraging Dynamic Blocks

Dynamic blocks can make your code less repetitive and easier to manage. For example, creating multiple ingress rules in a security group:

```
dynamic "ingress" {
 for_each = var.allowed_ports
 content {
 from_port = ingress.value["from_port"]
 to_port = ingress.value["to_port"]
 protocol = ingress.value["protocol"]
 cidr_blocks = ingress.value["cidr_blocks"]
```

```
}
}
```

Effective Use of Conditionals

Conditionals can be used to conditionally include/exclude resources or to set conditional values for attributes.

```
resource "aws_instance" "example" {
 count = var.create_instance ? 1 : 0
 ami = "ami-0c55b159cbfafe1f0"
 instance_type = "t2.micro"
}
```

File Organization for Modularity

Instead of placing all your code in one main.tf file, it's better to split it based on its function.

- main.tf: Calls modules and resource declarations.
- variables.tf: Variable declarations.
- outputs.tf: Output declarations.

Repository Structure

Make a separate directory for each environment such as dev, staging, and prod. Each should have its own main.tf, variables.tf, and outputs.tf. This enables environment isolation.

```
├── dev
│ ├── main.tf
│ ├── variables.tf
│ └── outputs.tf
```

```
├── staging
│ ├── main.tf
│ ├── variables.tf
│ └── outputs.tf
└── prod
 ├── main.tf
 ├── variables.tf
 └── outputs.tf
```

Sample Program: Adopting Style Guidelines

Here we'll pretend CloudOptic is interested in creating a virtual private cloud (VPC) with both public and private subnets. First, we follow all of the aforementioned style rules when we create a vpc.tf file for VPC and subnet configurations as below:

File: vpc.tf

```
module "vpc" {
 source = "./modules/vpc"


 # Required
 cidr_block = var.cidr_block


 # Optional
 enable_dns_support = var.enable_dns_support
```

```
tags = merge(
local.default_tags,
{
Name = "CloudOptic-VPC"
}
)
}
```

The above sample program keeps required and optional parameters separate, includes meaningful comments, and uses both locals and variables efficiently.

Utilizing Reusable Modules

A collection of resource configurations for a certain service or function can be encapsulated in a reusable module. You may promote best practices like DRY (Don't Repeat Yourself) and make your IaC more modular and scalable by using these modules to package your Terraform code into manageable and reusable sections.

Why Reusable Modules?

- Just as in software design, modularity in IaC means breaking down a complex system into smaller, independent modules that can be developed, changed, and scaled independently.
- Reusable modules enforce a consistent way of setting up resources. This standardization minimizes the chance of errors and ensures a uniform architecture.
- Once a module is created for a particular resource setup, it can be used in different projects or across different environments. This speeds up development time significantly.
- Using a module is as easy as calling it in your configuration, providing the required inputs, and Terraform will take care of the rest.
- Terraform's public module registry hosts a plethora of community-driven modules that can be used out of the box. This extends the capability of your projects without reinventing the wheel.

- Terraform modules can be versioned, allowing you to use different versions for different environments or even different microservices within the same environment.

Anatomy of a Module

In its simplest form, a module is a directory containing a set of .tf files. These files contain the resource definitions that are bundled as a module.

A typical structure might look like:

```
my-module/
│
├── main.tf # Main configuration file for the module
├── variables.tf # Variable declarations
└── outputs.tf # Output values
```

Sample Program: Reusable Module

So, you're using CloudOptic to set up virtual private clouds (VPCs) in a number of different contexts. This is one possible layout for a reusable VPC module that has all the necessary logic and configurations to set up a VPC:

modules/vpc/main.tf

```
resource "aws_vpc" "this" {
 cidr_block = var.cidr_block
 tags = var.tags
}
```

modules/vpc/variables.tf

```
variable "cidr_block" {
```

```
 description = "CIDR block for the VPC"
 type = string
}
variable "tags" {
 description = "Tags for the VPC"
 type = map(string)
}
```

You could then use this module in various environments like so:

dev/main.tf

```
module "dev_vpc" {
 source = "../modules/vpc"
 cidr_block = "10.0.0.0/16"
 tags = {
 Name = "dev-vpc"
 Environment = "Development"
 }
}
```

prod/main.tf

```
module "prod_vpc" {
 source = "../modules/vpc"
```

```
cidr_block = "192.168.0.0/16"

tags = {

Name = "prod-vpc"

Environment = "Production"

}

}
```

In this manner, you are achieving a high degree of reuse and maintainability. When the time comes to make a change, you modify the module, and those changes get propagated wherever the module is used, ensuring consistency.

Modules can also have:

- Local Values: These are akin to local variables within modules and help you simplify complex expressions.
- Dynamic Nested Blocks: If your module needs to create a dynamic number of similar resources, or resources with similar settings, dynamic nested blocks can help.
- Provisioners and Providers: Just like you can specify provisioners and providers in your main Terraform configuration, you can specify them within a module as well.

Extending VPC Module to Include EC2

We will take the previous example and apply it to a more outcome-focused task: configuring CloudOptic's EC2 instance inside a VPC.

The first step is to add an EC2 instance to our current VPC module. Below is an enhanced version of your modules/vpc/main.tf file:

```
resource "aws_vpc" "this" {

 cidr_block = var.cidr_block

 tags = var.tags

}

resource "aws_instance" "this" {
```

```
ami = var.ami_id
instance_type = var.instance_type
tags = merge(
{
"Name" = "my-instance"
},
var.tags
)
vpc_security_group_ids = [aws_security_group.this.id]
}
resource "aws_security_group" "this" {
name_prefix = "sg-"
vpc_id = aws_vpc.this.id
}
```

Corresponding changes in modules/vpc/variables.tf:

```
variable "ami_id" {
description = "AMI ID for EC2 instance"
type = string
}
variable "instance_type" {
description = "EC2 instance type"
```

```
type = string
}
```

Creating Module Instances for Different Environments

Just as before, you can create different Terraform configurations for development, staging, and production, each calling the same module but with different variables.

For instance, your dev/main.tf could look like this:

```
module "dev_infra" {
source = "../modules/vpc"
cidr_block = "10.0.0.0/16"
ami_id = "ami-123456"
instance_type= "t2.micro"
tags = {
Name = "dev-infra"
Environment = "Development"
}
}
```

Your prod/main.tf might differ:

```
module "prod_infra" {
source = "../modules/vpc"
cidr_block = "192.168.0.0/16"
ami_id = "ami-789012"
```

```
instance_type = "t2.large"
 tags = {
 Name = "prod-infra"
 Environment = "Production"
 }
}
```

Versioning Modules

One further useful feature is module versioning. Think about a scenario where you've updated your module with some improvements, yet these updates could cause some problems. You have the option to create many versions of your module and make them accessible to different settings. By doing so, you can ensure stability while progressively rolling out modifications.

```
module "prod_infra" {
 source = "../modules/vpc"
 version = "1.0.0"
 // ... other variables ...
}
```

Count and For_each in Modules

In the production environment, you can create several instances, but in the development environment, you can only create one. For this, you can use the module-level for_each or count parameters. These are in handy especially when you need to duplicate or conditionally include resources.

```
module "prod_infra" {
 source = "../modules/vpc"
```

```
count = 3 // Creates three instances of this module

  // ... other variables ...

}
```

Your Terraform projects will be more adaptable, scalable, and easy to maintain after you implement these techniques. In addition to saving time, reusable modules standardize setups and decrease the likelihood of errors.

Isolated Environments

Understanding Concept

Within the framework of IaC and Terraform, isolated environments provide a separate space for managing, testing, and deploying applications and services. You can keep development, staging, and production completely independent from one another with their help. For safer development and deployment cycles, the objective is to ensure that changes in one environment don't accidentally impact another.

Remote work spaces are essential for a big company like CloudOptic that may deal with sensitive customer data, real-time analytics, and other forms of data. A development environment is the initial point at which newly written code or features are tested and approved by developers. All new codes are tested in this isolated space. After passing development, the code is transferred to a staging environment that is highly similar to production. Strict testing and fine-tuning of performance are the main points here. The code is then moved into the production environment and made available to end-users after passing all tests.

Resources such as databases, application servers, load balancers, and caching servers can vary in setup and access regulations across various settings. It is possible to test these intricate configurations to a finer degree in isolated situations. In contrast to the production environment, which connects to the real, sensitive database, the development environment may communicate with a mock database.

Sample Program: Establishing Isolated Environment

Workspaces provide a simple method for managing separate environments in Terraform. The first step is to pretend that CloudOptic already has a standard environment defined by a base Terraform configuration as below:

```
provider "aws" {
```

```
 region = var.region
}
resource "aws_instance" "web" {
 count = var.instance_count
 ami = var.ami
 instance_type = var.instance_type
 // ... more configurations ...
}
```

In this basic setup, we have an AWS provider and an EC2 instance configuration. The variables region, instance_count, ami, and instance_type will differ from one environment to another.

To create isolated workspaces for development, staging, and production, you would execute:

```
terraform workspace new development
terraform workspace new staging
terraform workspace new production
```

Switch between them using:

```
terraform workspace select development
```

Now, you can maintain a terraform.tfvars file for each workspace, containing the specific variables:

development.tfvars

```
region = "us-west-2"
instance_count = 1
```

```
ami = "ami-dev"

instance_type = "t2.micro"staging.tfvarsregion = "us-east-1"

instance_count = 2

ami = "ami-stage"

instance_type = "t2.small"
```

To apply these, you can run:

```
terraform apply -var-file=development.tfvars
```

Additionally, each resource in each environment can have tags or naming conventions that tie it back to the environment.

For instance:

```
resource "aws_instance" "web" {

 //... other configs ...


 tags = {

 "Name" = "web-${terraform.workspace}"

 "Environment" = terraform.workspace

 }

}
```

Here we have covered the basics of setting up separate environments with Terraform workspaces and specific variable files. This configuration allows for safer testing and deployment strategies by ensuring that modifications to one environment do not affect the others.

Separate Directories vs. Isolated Workspaces

An additional option for managing numerous environments with Terraform is to use separate directories instead of separated workspaces. Unlike workspaces, which use the same configuration to toggle between states in order to isolate environments, directories use different Terraform configurations for each environment.

In this section, we will delve into both the theoretical underpinnings and a more realistic strategy.

Understanding Separate Directories

In the separate directory approach, you maintain independent directories—each with its Terraform files and states—for development, staging, and production. There is no sharing or overlapping of configurations or state files between these environments, making them utterly isolated by design. Each directory can be treated as its self-contained Terraform project.

This method allows for greater customization and fewer chances of accidental modifications affecting multiple environments. On the flip side, it can lead to some redundancy and requires extra effort to keep the common elements in sync across directories. However, that is a manageable trade-off for the additional security and customization it offers.

Sample Program: Separate Directories vs. Workspaces

To further understand, we will pretend that CloudOptic or we wish to oversee a group of AWS EC2 instances belonging to the Analytics, DevOps, and Customer Service divisions. A little different configuration, including instance size, software packages, and security settings, is needed for each department.

Directory Structure

In the separate directory approach, your directory structure might look something like this:

```
├── analytics
│ ├── main.tf
│ ├── variables.tf
│ └── terraform.tfstate
├── devops
│ ├── main.tf
│ ├── variables.tf
```

```
│ └── terraform.tfstate
└── customer_service
 ├── main.tf
 ├── variables.tf
 └── terraform.tfstate
```

Each directory has its main.tf describing the infrastructure setup, variables.tf containing environment-specific variables, and terraform.tfstate that holds the state of the resources for that specific environment.

In the analytics/main.tf, you might specify EC2 instances optimized for data processing:

```
resource "aws_instance" "analytics_instance" {
 instance_type = "m5.large"
 // ... other configs tailored for analytics ...
}
```

Meanwhile, in devops/main.tf, the instances might be optimized for CI/CD workflows:

```
resource "aws_instance" "devops_instance" {
 instance_type = "t3.medium"
 // ... other configs tailored for DevOps ...
}
```

Risk Mitigation

With separate directories, there is no chance of accidentally applying changes to the wrong environment by forgetting to switch workspaces, which is a risk with the workspace approach. Each directory can be secured and accessed based on the requirement. For instance, only the DevOps team might have the permission to make changes in the devops directory.

Synchronization Challenge

While customization is a strong point, it also means that if you have common configurations or modules that need to be updated, you'll have to do it in every directory. For instance, if CloudOptic decides to switch to a different AMI for all Linux instances, this change would need to be made in each directory's main.tf.

Version Control

Since each directory is its distinct entity, it allows for easy integration with version control systems. Each environment can have its separate branch, making rollbacks or feature testing easier and safer.

The separate directory strategy for managing environments aligns well with the principles of complete isolation and granular control. It allows one to tailor each department's infrastructure to its specific needs while keeping the environments strictly separated. This approach, although requiring more upfront setup and ongoing synchronization, pays off in the form of reduced risk and increased customization.

Performance and Scalability Indicators

There are a lot of moving parts in Terraform that affect its performance and scalability, including the design, resource allocation, and maintenance of state files. These factors are going to be more important to think about when your infrastructure expands.

We will analyze:

Scalability Indicators

Resource Utilization

Tracking CPU, memory, and network utilization helps identify potential bottlenecks. If CloudOptic observes that a resource, such as an EC2 instance, consistently runs at 90% CPU utilization, it's a clear indicator that you need to scale up or out.

Infrastructure Elasticity

This relates to how quickly your infrastructure can adapt to workload changes. For instance, if CloudOptic' data analytics workloads are scheduled for month-end, the infrastructure should be able to scale up swiftly to handle this and scale down afterward.

Queue Depth

When dealing with data pipelines or message queues like AWS SQS, an increasing queue depth indicates that the system is receiving more data than it can process. This is a vital scalability metric, as neglecting it could lead to data loss or increased latency.

Performance Indicators

Latency

The time it takes to fulfill a request should be minimal. If CloudOptic uses an API Gateway, latency should be consistently low. Any spikes could indicate an issue with the service or underlying resources that may need immediate attention.

Throughput

This measures the number of operations a system can handle in a given time. For example, if CloudOptic runs a database that starts to have a significantly reduced throughput, this could be an indicator of a need for optimization or scaling.

Error Rates

High error rates usually indicate performance issues. Whether it's 4xx or 5xx HTTP status codes from an API or missed deadlines in a data processing job, these are usually indicative of underlying problems.

Practical Measures for CloudOptic

Auto-Scaling Groups

CloudOptic could use AWS Auto Scaling Groups or similar services in other cloud providers to automatically adjust the number of active instances. This is particularly useful for applications with variable workloads, ensuring that you're neither over-provisioning nor under-provisioning resources.

State Backends

State management can become complicated as CloudOptic scales. Using a dedicated backend like Amazon S3 with state locking and encryption can improve performance by ensuring only one operation alters the state at a time.

Resource Tagging

This may seem simple, but as you scale, it becomes invaluable for tracking costs and optimizing usage. By implementing a consistent tagging strategy from the get-go, CloudOptic can more easily identify where optimizations can be made.

Code Reviews

CloudOptic should regularly review Terraform configurations and modules, keeping an eye on deprecated resources or practices. This proactive measure helps in early identification of possible performance bottlenecks.

Parallelization and Workspaces

Terraform can perform actions in parallel to speed up execution. If CloudOptic has multiple environments (e.g., staging, production), utilizing Terraform workspaces can isolate state files, allowing teams to work in parallel without conflicts, thereby increasing efficiency.

Caching and Content Delivery

For applications with global user bases, CloudOptic could use services like AWS CloudFront to cache content closer to the end-users. This reduces latency and improves the speed of content delivery.

Monitoring and Alerts

CloudOptic should integrate monitoring tools like AWS CloudWatch or Grafana to keep an eye on the performance indicators. Setting up alerts for unusual spikes in resource utilization or error rates can provide early warnings before issues become critical.

If CloudOptic monitors these metrics and follows best practices, it can guarantee that its Terraform-managed infrastructure is elastic and runs at peak efficiency. Instead than responding to problems, which usually causes downtime or less-than-ideal performance, the emphasis should always be on proactively finding and fixing such problems.

Integrating Terraform with CDKTF

The Cloud Development Kit for Terraform (CDKTF) allows you to define cloud infrastructure using familiar programming languages such as TypeScript, Python, and Java. In this case, we will consider how CloudOptic could integrate an existing Terraform-based infrastructure with CDKTF.

Install CDKTF CLI

First, you need to install the CDKTF CLI by running:

```
npm install -g cdktf-cli
```

Initialize New CDKTF Project

Create a new directory and initialize a new CDKTF project with:

```
cdktf init --template="typescript" --local
```

Here, I am using TypeScript as the language, but you can choose other supported languages. The --local flag tells CDKTF to use a local Terraform CLI for deployments.

Generate Constructs

CloudOptic has a VPC and an EC2 instance managed via Terraform. You can import these into your CDKTF application using:

```
cdktf get
```

This downloads the necessary providers and creates a generated constructs directory. Then, in your main TypeScript file, you can use these constructs.

Reference Existing Resources

You can't directly import state into CDKTF, but you can reference existing resources. Let us say your VPC ID in Terraform state is vpc-12345. You can refer to it in your CDKTF code like:

```
const vpc = Vpc.fromVpcAttributes(this, 'ImportedVPC', {

 vpcId: 'vpc-12345',

});
```

Add New Resources

Add a new S3 bucket via CDKTF, for example:

```
new S3Bucket(this, 'MyBucket', {

 bucket: 'my-bucket',

});
```

Synthesize

Run the cdktf synth command to synthesize the TypeScript code into Terraform JSON configuration.

To ensure your existing infrastructure will not be impacted adversely, you can run:

```
cdktf diff
```

This will show you what changes will be made to your existing infrastructure.

CDKTF Deploy

If everything looks good, deploy your resources using:

```
cdktf deploy
```

After successful deployment, you should see the new S3 bucket in your AWS Console, confirming the successful integration of Terraform and CDKTF.

Make Iterative Changes

Make some changes to your CDKTF code, for instance, add an additional tag to your S3 bucket, and run cdktf diff and cdktf deploy again.

Verifying that the new modifications did not impact the current resources is of the utmost importance. To validate the infrastructure state, it may be necessary to monitor logs, examine resource properties, or execute automation tests.

Precautions

Knowing how CloudOptic's resources are currently interdependent is critical. Any modification to a security group that is linked to an already-existing EC2 instance, for instance, may have an effect on that instance. To understand the impact, run cdktf diff every time.

Integration of existing Terraform-managed resources with a CDKTF application isn't just a 'set-and-forget' process. It's an ongoing commitment to manage and monitor your infrastructure diligently.

Summary

We covered advanced Terraform practices in this chapter that can help you manage your infrastructure more efficiently. By following the guidelines laid out in the Terraform Style Guide, we were able to demonstrate how scripts written using Terraform may be safer to run and easier to maintain. Practical code snippets were used to exemplify this point, highlighting the importance of a well-structured Terraform codebase and how important it is in relation to the infrastructure it controls. We also delved into the idea of reusable modules, which can streamline code and facilitate the management of extensive infrastructure. We took a look at how development and deployment processes can be accelerated by developing modules for commonly used resources, such as VPC and EC2 instances.

Isolation of the environment was another important aspect. By limiting the impact of changes, environment isolation enables effective risk management, as demonstrated in the CloudOptic scenario. We covered many approaches, like creating distinct directories and working in separate workspaces, to divide up environments for development, testing, and production. This keeps potentially disastrous modifications from wreaking havoc on the entire system and instead keeps them localized to a single area.

We also learned performance and scalability metrics, stressing the importance of modular architecture and effective resource allocation. To be scalable, a system must be able to both expand as needed and shrink as needed to maximize efficiency and minimize expenses. Lastly, we integrated CDKTF with existing Terraform infrastructure through a thorough practical exercise. More leeway in specifying and controlling cloud resources is yours with this integration, which combines the strength of Terraform with the expressive potential of programming languages provided by CDKTF.

By the time you finish this chapter or rather this entire book, you should have all the information you need to put these advanced Terraform principles into action, making it easier for you to manage complicated cloud infrastructures. Among these skills is the ability to integrate state-of-the-art tools like CDKTF to expand your Terraform capabilities, as well as the ability to keep your codebase clean, optimize for reusability, isolate environments, and maintain scalability.

Test Exercise

1. What is the standard file extension for a Terraform variable definition file?
    a. .tfvars
    b. .tf
    c. .terraform
    d. .var
2. Which command would you use to initialize the modules before running any other Terraform command?
    a. terraform plan
    b. terraform apply
    c. terraform init
    d. terraform get
3. In the context of CloudOptic, what does environment isolation primarily aim to achieve?
    a. Cost-saving
    b. Risk containment
    c. Code reusability
    d. Performance optimization
4. Which approach would allow you to share state files between different environments?
    a. Separate Directories
    b. Isolated Workspaces
    c. Both A and B
    d. Neither A nor B

5. What aspect does vertical scaling address in a CloudOptic environment?
    a. Increasing the number of instances
    b. Improving the capability of a single instance
    c. Decreasing the number of instances
    d. Networking optimization
6. What is one of the benefits of integrating CDKTF with Terraform?
    a. Eliminates the need for a Terraform installation
    b. Adds multi-language support
    c. Replaces Terraform entirely
    d. None of the above
7. Which command is used to automatically format your Terraform code?
    a. terraform validate
    b. terraform fmt
    c. terraform lint
    d. terraform refresh
8. If you have defined an output within a module, how do you access it in your main Terraform configuration?
    a. module.<MODULE_NAME>.<OUTPUT_NAME>
    b. output.<OUTPUT_NAME>
    c. terraform output <OUTPUT_NAME>
    d. module-output.<MODULE_NAME>.<OUTPUT_NAME>
9. Which command allows you to apply a configuration change to only a specific resource?
    a. terraform apply -target=resource_type.resource_name
    b. terraform plan -target=resource_type.resource_name
    c. Both A and B
    d. Neither A nor B
10. Which command can be used to manually edit the state file?
    a. terraform state pull
    b. terraform state push
    c. terraform state edit
    d. terraform state rm

Index

T

V

W

Epilogue

It is our sincere wish that by the time you reach the end of this book, you will have not only gained knowledge, but also been completely changed - a Terraform expert ready to take on any challenge in infrastructure. We set out on this adventure with the intention of providing an all-inclusive, practical guide to Terraform, detailing its fundamental design and all of its advanced features. Our goal in creating this book was to make it as thorough and applicable to real life as possible by using a combination of theoretical ideas and practical examples with the backdrop of CloudOptic Solutions.

No matter your level of experience as a developer, you will find this content both interesting and challenging because each chapter builds on the previous one. Before delving into modules and dependencies, we covered the fundamentals, such as providers, resources, and state files. We have successfully navigated the complex situations of state manipulation, configuration drift handling, scaling, and performance issues. Your training has prepared you not just for the theoretical but also for the practical and industry-specific tasks that lie ahead. However, being an expert with a program like Terraform is an ongoing process, not an endpoint. Just like every other technological landscape, Terraform is always changing. Although this book lays a solid groundwork, it is essential to stay current with the latest features, best practices, and community contributions if you want to remain relevant. With a wealth of knowledge and enthusiasm, the HashiCorp community is always looking to expand Terraform's capabilities. Participate in this group, teach others what you know, and keep learning so that you can all advance.

In addition, infrastructure and DevOps ecosystems are bigger than Terraform. A great way to broaden your expertise is to study how to connect Terraform to various languages, platforms, and tools. There are a lot of people here who could be interested in learning more about CDKTF integration or sophisticated approaches to state management and version control. Other people may be more concerned with the governance, cost control, and compliance aspects of scaling Terraform processes throughout a big organization.

Being able to apply one's knowledge is the ultimate litmus test. Putting your newfound knowledge to use in a practical setting is the next best thing. Your newly acquired skills can be put to use in any endeavor, no matter how big or little. The goal of the exercises and quizzes has been to get you ready for this by providing a challenge and an opportunity for self-evaluation. You have all the necessary tools to achieve your goals, whether it's implementing an enterprise-wide IaC project or attempting to become certified by HashiCorp in Terraform.

Your participation in this learning experience is greatly appreciated. All sorts of doors will open for you in the future thanks to the skills you've picked up. The time has come for you to put them into practice; after all, coming up with new ideas is the surest method to know what's coming.

Thank You

www.ingramcontent.com/pod-product-compliance
Lightning Source LLC
Chambersburg PA
CBHW080212170726
48282CB00030B/1092
9788119177295